GLOBE EDUCATION SHAKESPEARE

FOR **AQA** GCSE ENGLISH LITERATURE

MACBETH

William Shakespeare

HODDER EDUCATION
AN HACHETTE UK COMPANY

Shakespeare and the Globe

Shakespeare was born in 1564, in Stratford, a small town in the Midlands. We know he was still in Stratford as an eighteen-year old, when he got married. By 1592, he had moved to London, become an actor, and become a playwright. Shakespeare died in Stratford in 1616. He probably retired three or four years earlier, having bought land, and the biggest house in the town.

Shakespeare was successful. He became a shareholder in his acting company, and a shareholder in the Globe – the new theatre they built in 1599. His company was the best in the land, and the new king, James I, made them his company in 1603. They were known as the King's Men. Men, because women were not allowed to act on the stage. Boys or men played all the women's parts. Shakespeare wrote at least 40 plays, of which 38 survive. Only eighteen of his plays were printed in his lifetime, and *Macbeth* was not one of them. It only survives because, after his death, his colleagues published a collection of 36 of his plays, known as the *First Folio*.

London Theatres

There were professional companies of actors working in London from the middle of the sixteenth century. They usually performed in inns, and the city council often tried to ban them. The solution was to have their own purpose-built theatre, just outside the area the council controlled. The first, simply called *The Theatre*, opened in 1576.

Shakespeare's Globe today

Sam Wanamaker, an American actor and director, founded the Shakespeare's Globe Trust in 1970. Sam could not understand why there wasn't a proper memorial to the world's greatest playwright in the city where he had lived and worked. He started fundraising to build a new Globe Theatre. Sadly, Sam died before the theatre opened in 1997.

Heavens

Upper stage

Stage

Galleries

Entrances

Yard

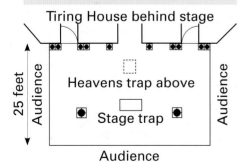

The stage trap opened into the area under the stage. The heavens trap was not on the stage, but above it. Actors playing gods might be lowered down to the stage through it.

The first Globe Theatre

The Globe Theatre was open-air. If it rained, some of the audience got wet. There was no special lighting; so the plays were performed in the afternoon, in daylight. This meant that, unlike most modern theatres, the actors could see the audience, as well as the audience see the actors (and each other). It may have held as many as 3,000 people, with, perhaps, 1,000 standing in the yard. Those standing paid one old penny (there were 240 in £1). The rest sat in the three galleries, so they were under cover if it rained. They paid more, at least two pence, and as much as six pence for the best seats. The audience was a mixture of social classes, with the poorer people standing.

The stage was large, and extended into the middle of the yard, so there were people on three sides. We think it had three entrances in the back wall – a door on either side, and a larger one in the middle. There was a roof so the actors, and their expensive costumes, would always be in the dry. The underside of this roof, called *the heavens*, was painted with the signs of the zodiac. There was also an upper stage, which was sometimes used in plays, sometimes used by the musicians, and also had the most expensive seats in the theatre. All the rest of the audience could see people who sat in the upper stage area. If you sat there, people could see who you were, that you could afford to sit there, and your expensive clothes.

The **play text** is the place to start. What characters say is in black, and stage directions are in blue. Line numbers, on the right, help you refer to an exact place.

	More loud knocking within.
	Anon, anon! I pray you, remember the porter.
	[He opens the door. Enter Macduff and Lennox.]
Macduff	Was it so late, friend, ere you went to bed, 20
	That you do lie so late?

Some **stage directions**, like the second one above, have square brackets. This means they are not in the original text, but have been added to help you when you read. They tell you what you would see on the stage.

> 64–5 **but as pictures … painted devil:** like 'scary' pictures that only children would fear

The **glossary** is right next to the text. To help you find the word or phrase you want, each entry has the line number in blue, then the word or phrase in black, and finally the explanation in blue again. To keep it clear, sometimes, as in this case, some words from the original have been missed out, and replaced with three dots.

Actor's view boxes are exactly what they say. Actors who have played the part at the Globe tell you what they thought about their character and some of their choices.

There are lots of **photos** of productions of the play at Shakespeare's Globe. You'll notice different productions look very different. This is because each creative team and cast interpret the text. And remember, Shakespeare wrote to be interpreted by actors, and to have his plays watched, not read. The captions (on green boxes) tell you what you are looking at, and give you a question to think about. Unless the question says otherwise, the answer will be in the play text on the opposite page. The names of the actors are in smaller print.

From the Rehearsal Room gives you versions of the exercises actors use during rehearsals to help them understand the play. They come with questions that help you reflect on what you can learn from the exercise. **Working Cuts** sometimes go with the From the Rehearsal Room activities. They cut lines from the scene so you can do the activity in the time you have available.

Shakespeare's World boxes give you important context for the play. For example, what most people at the time believed about witches is different from what most people believe today. If you understand the difference, it helps you to understand how the characters react to the Witches in the play.

Director's Notes boxes come at the end of every scene. They give you a quick summary of the most important things in the scene, and a focus to think about.

Looking forward to the Exam

To help you get ready for the exam, parts of the book are written by experienced examiners. Turn the page (to pages 6–7) to find a explanation of how the exam works. This is a good place to start. Then, while you are working on the play, there are two special features to help.

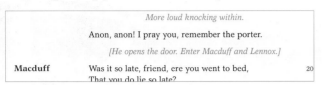

exam SKILLS

Target skill: analysing the presentation of character through dialogue

Question: How does Shakespeare present the changing relationship between Macbeth and Lady Macbeth in lines 15–67?

- Shakespeare had Duncan murdered offstage. The audience are probably more tense because they don't see it, but wait for news with Lady Macbeth.
- Lady Macbeth's feeling that Duncan "resembled my father as he slept" will come back to haunt her.
- Sleep and death were closely linked in the minds of Jacobean audiences.

With a partner, decide whether you agree with, disagree with, or are uncertain about the statements below.

1 Lady Macbeth needed drink to get false courage.
2 Macbeth's hands are covered in blood and his mind is at breaking point.
3 The questions and very short sentences in lines 20–28 between Macbeth and Lady Macbeth reveal their nervous uncertainty.
4 Lady Macbeth is the stronger of the two since her presence of mind prevents instant discovery.

5 Macbeth's agony that he could not say "Amen" is because he knows he will be damned.
6 Thinking he heard the cry, "Sleep no more. Macbeth does murder sleep" shows that Macbeth has a conscience.
7 Saying "Consider it not so deeply" and "Who was it that thus cried?" shows that Lady Macbeth lacks imagination.
8 Because Macbeth feels overwhelmed by blood and guilt, the audience still feel sympathy for him.
9 Lady Macbeth's claim that "a little water clears us of this deed" is an example of dramatic irony.
10 Shakespeare uses the structure of this dialogue to show Lady Macbeth is the dominant partner.

Using your insights from this activity, how would you answer the question above?

Exam skills boxes focus on the skills you need to do well. They start by telling you the skill you are going to practice, then give you a question with some of the same demands as the question you will get in the exam. What follows is a mixture of explanation, example, and some things for you to think about and practice.

exam PREPARATION

Text Focus: Act 1 Scene 7 lines 28–83

This is a key scene in terms of structure and of the relationship between Macbeth and Lady Macbeth. It shows Lady Macbeth's power over herself and over her husband, since if she had not goaded him into it, Macbeth might have decided to "proceed no further in this business".

(AO1) Response to characters and events:
- In this scene Macbeth is not the "Bellona's bridegroom" of earlier scenes who acts almost without thinking. *How does Shakespeare show this?*
- Most audiences, because we are given insight into his fears about the "horrid deed" of killing his king, have some sympathy for Macbeth at this point. *What are your feelings about Macbeth and Lady Macbeth at this point in the play?*
- In lines 38–52 Lady Macbeth accuses Macbeth of being a coward and less than a man. *Which of her taunts do you think hurts him most? Explain your choice.*
- Lady Macbeth is the dominant figure, showing none of Macbeth's indecision. *What finally makes Macbeth change his mind?*

(AO2) Language, structure and form:
- Shakespeare deliberately showed Macbeth as a warrior before showing him as a worrier. *Why might he have done that?*

- Macbeth is now fearful of losing his reputation, of breaking the laws of loyalty and hospitality and of "deep damnation" in "the life to come". *Which images give the most telling insight into his fears?*
- Macbeth says so little and Lady Macbeth says so much during this scene. *Why might Shakespeare have written the scene in this way?*
- *What words do Lady Macbeth and Macbeth use to refer to killing the king, and why is 'murder' not one of them?*

(AO3) Context and ideas:
- Lady Macbeth declares that she would have plucked her nipple from the boneless gums of her child "and dashed the brains out, had I so sworn as you have done to this." *How does this make you feel about Lady Macbeth? Do you think there would be a difference between the effect these lines have on modern audiences, and audiences in Shakespeare's time?*
- In the kingdom of James I unity and stability were fragile, and Guy Fawkes was recently executed when the play was first performed. *Why might this have made killing a king seem more terrible to Shakespeare's original audience?*

Question:
How is the relationship between Macbeth and Lady Macbeth presented in this scene? Include evidence from the text to justify your view.

Exam preparation boxes help you practice for the exam. Your exam question starts with an extract from the play, and here you can see you are given a text focus, with about 40 lines. Read these lines first and carefully (just like you will need to read the extract first and carefully in the exam).

In the Exam your answer will be marked against three objectives (see pages 6–7). Here you are shown some of the sorts of things you can do for each objective, and given some ideas to think about and practice on. Finally you get the question, which is like one of the different types of question as you will get in the exam. With the work and thinking you have done before, you will be in a good position to answer it.

The Characters in the play

This book uses photographs from four productions of *Macbeth* at Shakespeare's Globe. The actors and creative teams of each production are an important part of the book.

	2001 *Director:* *Tim Carroll*	spring 2010 *Director:* *Bill Buckhurst*	summer 2010 *Director:* *Lucy Bailey*	2013 *Director:* *Eve Best*
Duncan, king of Scotland	Terry McGinty	Andrew Whipp	James Clyde	Gawn Grainger
Malcolm, his son	Chu Omambala	Philip Cumbus	James McArdle	Philip Cumbus
Donalbain, his son	Mark Springer	Shane Zaza	Craig Vye	Colin Ryan
Macbeth, a general	Jasper Britton	James Garnon	Elliot Cowan	Joseph Millson
Lady Macbeth	Eve Best	Claire Cox	Laura Rogers	Samantha Spiro
Banquo, a general	Patrick Brennan	Matt Costain	Christian Bradley	Billy Boyd
Fleance, his son	Mark Springer	Rachel Winters	Josh Swinney James Beesley	Colin Ryan
Macduff, a nobleman	Liam Brennan	Nicholas Khan	Keith Dunphy	Stuart Bowman
Lady Macduff	Hilary Tones	Karen Bryson	Simone Kirby	Finty Williams
Son of the Macduffs		Liam Brennan	Austin Moulton Charlie George	Colin Ryan
Lennox, a nobleman	Richard Attlee	Rachel Winters	Nick Court	Harry Hepple
Ross, a nobleman	Jonathan Oliver		Julius D'Silva	Geoff Aymer
Menteith, a nobleman			Michael Camp	
Angus, a nobleman	Jan Knightley		Ian Pirie	
Caithness, a nobleman				
Siward, an English soldier		Andrew Whipp	Ken Shorter	
Young Siward, his son		Shane Zaza	Craig Vye	
English Doctor				
Scottish Doctor	Terry McGinty		Ian Pirie	Gawn Grainger
Captain, a soldier	Colin Hurley	Russell Layton	Michael Camp	Harry Hepple
Porter	Paul Chahidi	Russell Layton	Frank Scantori	Bette Bourne
Old Man			Ken Shorter	
First Witch	Liza Hayden	Karen Bryson	Janet Fullerlove	Moyo Akandé
Second Witch	Paul Chahidi	Rachel Winters	Karen Anderson	Jess Murphy
Third Witch	Colin Hurley	Shane Zaza	Simone Kirby	Cat Simmons
Hecate				
Seyton	Paul Chahidi	Matt Costain	James Clyde	Jonathan Chambers
First Murderer	Jan Knightley	Nicholas Khan	Michael Camp	Geoff Aymer
Second Murderer	Richard Attlee	Philip Cumbus	Craig Vye	Harry Hepple
Third Murderer		Andrew Whipp		
Gentlewoman	Hilary Tones		Janet Fullerlove	
Lords, Gentlemen, Soldiers, Attendants, Messengers				
Designer	Laura Hopkins	Isla Shaw	Katrina Lindsay	Mike Britton
Composer	Claire van Kampen	Olly Fox	Orlando Gough	Olly Fox
Choreographer	Siân Williams	Siân Williams	Javier de Frutos	Charlotte Broom
Fight Director		Alison de Burgh	Philip D'Orleans	Kevin McCurdy
Musical Director	Claire van Kampen	Genevieve Williams	Belinda Sykes	Phil Hopkins

exam PREPARATION

GCSE examiners are clear about what they expect students to do when responding to questions about a Shakespeare play. These expectations are set out in the general Assessment Objectives for English Literature, outlined in 'teacherspeak' below.

ASSESSMENT OBJECTIVES FOR GCSE ENGLISH LITERATURE

AO	EXPECTATION	WEIGHTING
AO1	Read, understand and respond to texts. Students should be able to: • maintain a critical style and develop an informed personal response • use textual references, including quotations, to support and illustrate interpretations.	15%
AO2	Analyse the language, form and structure used by a writer to create meanings and effects, using relevant subject terminology where appropriate.	15%
AO3	Show understanding of the relationship between texts and the contexts in which they were written.	7.5%
AO4	Use a range of vocabulary and sentence structures for clarity, purpose and effect, with accurate spelling and punctuation.	2.5%

Below is a summary of what these general assessment objectives mean for you when being examined on *Macbeth*. You will recognise the headings from the Exam Preparation boxes in this Globe edition.

AO1 Response to characters and events
• write about your personal response to aspects of plot, characterisation, events and settings
• offer your personal exploration (not just an explanation) of why Shakespeare made the choices that he did about characters, events and ideas
• comment in detail on characters' motivation, the sequence of events, and how one action on stage is linked with others
• make an informed personal response based on your analysis and evaluation of the text
• support your point of view by quoting the text or referring to events in the play.

(AO2) Language, structure and form
• write in detail about language, using appropriate linguistic and literary terminology e.g. soliloquy, blank verse, rhyming couplets, denouement
• show your understanding of words, phrases or sentences in context by explaining the impact that they could have on an audience
• distinguish between what is stated explicitly and what is implied, and explain the difference this makes to listeners
• evaluate (not just praise) Shakespeare's choice of vocabulary, his use of imagery and his poetic techniques
• analyse and evaluate how dramatic structure and dramatic form contribute to the impact of the play.

(AO3) Context and ideas
• show that you understand how the ideas in the text link with each other and with the chronological context in which it was written

• identify themes and distinguish between them
• demonstrate that you recognise that different interpretations and different responses to a text are possible
• use your understanding of Shakespeare's time, society and cultural context to inform your evaluation of the play and its impact on different audiences.

As a student of *Macbeth* for AQA:
• Remember that all the questions, and the mark scheme, are constructed around these Assessment Objectives.
• Relax, because there will not be a sudden and unexpected change in the style of questioning: the examiners have to ensure every year that all the Assessment Objectives can be assessed through the examination paper and that the paper is similar in format to the examples published on the AQA website.
• Recognise that all the Assessment Objectives matter, but some matter more than others – AO1 and AO2 carry the most marks.

• Realise that the question on Macbeth will be marked out of 34 marks, with 4 of those marks allocated for accurate spelling, punctuation and grammar.

Question format
Questions on Paper 1 will be based on an extract of 20–30 lines from *Macbeth* and have two bullet points:

1 You will be asked to comment on the presentation of some aspect of the extract e.g. character, theme or dramatic technique.

2 You will be asked about the presentation of that same aspect in relation to the play as a whole.

You will have 45 minutes to complete the question on Macbeth. It will be set out like the example on the next page.

exam PREPARATION

Starting with this extract, explain how far you think Shakespeare presents Macbeth as a weak character.

Write about:
- **how Shakespeare presents Macbeth in this extract.**
- **how Shakespeare presents Macbeth in the play as a whole.**

Remember that the first bullet point will ask you to write about the extract and the second bullet point will require you to write about the play as a whole.

How to respond to a question
- Spend about 5 minutes reading the passage and the question carefully. Underline or highlight the key words in the question and the bullet points.
- Spend approximately 20 minutes responding to each bullet point, remembering to comment on the three main Assessment Objectives.
- Draw on your knowledge of the whole play in order to comment fully on any particular part of it.
- Plan your answer:
  1 Decide on your main line of argument.
  2 Arrange the supporting points in relation to your argument.
  3 Think of textual evidence (brief quotations) to support your points.
  4 Write your introduction with your conclusion in mind.

Key points to bear in mind
- Questions are usually about Shakespeare and his methods (language, structure, form) rather than about characters.
- Your answer needs to be focused firmly on the question. Only a relevant response will gain substantial marks.
- Keep quotations short, but try to use them to clinch every point you make.
- We learn about characters from what they say and do, from what is said to them and what is said about them.
- Be ready to present your own ideas, feelings and reactions, but make sure that your opinions are always backed up by evidence from the play.
- Language is relevant to every question, so make sure that you write about particular words and phrases and the impact they might have on an audience.
- Shakespeare's original audiences would have differed from a modern audience in ideas and attitudes.
- Answers are marked for the accuracy of your written English.

Examiners use a complex markscheme to help them grade answers. Here is a simpler version outlining what you need to do for a good or very good answer. Answer the final question in any Exam Preparation box, and try marking your own answers against the criteria below.

For your answer to be good (i.e. grade 4/5) it would need to be clear, relevant to the task, detailed and developed. This means:

AO1
- offering a thoughtful, relevant response to the whole task
- demonstrating clear understanding of the play through the use of detailed references and quotation
- developing a clear line of argument

AO2
- using literary terms and evidence from the text to explain Shakespeare's methods as a writer in terms of language, structure and dramatic form
- explaining how Shakespeare's methods might affect different audiences

AO3
- considering ideas and contextual factors which might have influenced Shakespeare or his audiences
- explaining links between the task, the text and the context of the play as a whole

For your answer to be very good (i.e. grade 1/2) it would need to be sophisticated in style, structure and content. This means offering a complete, intelligent and individual response to the task by:

AO1
- developing a personal interpretation of the text in relation to the task.
- structuring a personal and perceptive line of argument
- using subtly chosen textual references and quotations
- exploring ideas imaginatively

AO2
- using critical terms precisely to analyse Shakespeare's language, structure and dramatic form
- exploring the impact of Shakespeare's methods on audiences from different cultures and times

AO3
- linking the play intelligently with Shakespeare's context
- exploring themes and ideas in relation to different perspectives and interpretations

The three Witches from the spring 2010 production.

Why do you think Shakespeare chooses to start the play with the Witches?

l–r, Shane Zaza, Karen Bryson, Rachel Winters

ACT 1 SCENE 1

Thunder and lightning. Enter three Witches.

First Witch	When shall we three meet again?
	In thunder, lightning, or in rain?
Second Witch	When the hurly-burly's done,
	When the battle's lost and won.
Third Witch	That will be ere the set of sun.
First Witch	Where the place?
Second Witch	Upon the heath.
Third Witch	There to meet with Macbeth.
First Witch	I come, Graymalkin!
Second Witch	Paddock calls.
Third Witch	Anon.
All	Fair is foul, and foul is fair:
	Hover through the fog and filthy air.

(line 5)
(line 10)

Exit all three.

ACT 1 SCENE 2

Noise of battle offstage, including drums and trumpets. Enter King Duncan, Malcolm, Donalbain, Lennox, with attendants, meeting a bleeding captain.

Duncan	What bloody man is that? He can report,
	As seemeth by his plight, of the revolt
	The newest state.
Malcolm	This is the sergeant,
	Who like a good and hardy soldier fought
	'Gainst my captivity. — Hail, brave friend!
	Say to the king the knowledge of the broil
	As thou didst leave it.
Captain	Doubtful it stood,
	As two spent swimmers, that do cling together
	And choke their art. The merciless Macdonald
	(Worthy to be a rebel, for to that
	The multiplying villainies of nature
	Do swarm upon him) from the Western Isles
	Of kerns and gallowglasses is supplied.
	And Fortune, on his damnèd quarrel smiling,
	Showed like a rebel's whore. But all's too weak,
	For brave Macbeth (well he deserves that name)
	Disdaining Fortune, with his brandished steel
	Which smoked with bloody execution,
	Like Valour's minion, carved out his passage
	Till he faced the slave:
	Which ne'er shook hands, nor bade farewell to him,

(line 5)
(line 10)
(line 15)
(line 20)

Director's Note, 1.1

✔ The play starts in noise and mystery.
✔ The Witches plan to meet Macbeth.

---

3 **hurly-burly:** fighting
5 **ere:** before
6 **heath:** flat, open, windswept countryside
8-9 **Graymalkin/Paddock:** two of the Witches' three 'familiars' – their link to the world of magic, disguised as animals. Graymalkin is a cat, Paddock a toad. They are calling the Witches away
10 **Anon:** I'll be there straight away

1-3 **He can ... newest state:** He's come from the battlefield so can tell us what's happened
4 **hardy:** brave
5 **'Gainst my captivity:** to stop me being captured
6 **broil:** battle
7 **Doubtful it stood:** the outcome of the battle was uncertain
8 **spent:** exhausted
9 **choke their art:** stop each other from swimming
11–12 **The multiplying villainies ... upon him):** he has so many bad qualities
13 **kerns:** lightly armed foot soldiers
13 **gallowglasses:** soldiers armed with axes
14–5 **And Fortune ... rebel's whore:** And Fortune (the goddess of luck) sided with Macdonald, giving the rebels luck the way a prostitute gives her body
15 **all's too weak:** Fortune and the troops were not strong enough
17 **Disdaining:** disregarding
17 **brandished steel:** drawn sword
18 **smoked with bloody execution:** steamed with newly-shed blood
19 **Valour:** bravery
19 **minion:** favourite, chosen person
19 **carved out his passage:** hacked his way through to Macdonald
20 **slave:** used to show contempt for Macdonald

Till he unseamed him from the nave to the chops,
And fixed his head upon our battlements.

Duncan   O valiant cousin, worthy gentleman!

Captain   As whence the sun 'gins his reflection,
Shipwrecking storms and direful thunders,
So from that spring, whence comfort seemed to come,
Discomfort swells. Mark, King of Scotland, mark.
No sooner justice had, with valour armed,
Compelled these skipping kerns to trust their heels,

22 **unseamed him ... to the chops:** slashed him open from his navel to his jaw

24 **cousin:** Macbeth is related to Duncan

25 25–8 **As whence ... Discomfort swells:** Just as the sun can be replaced by storms, so seeming help can be replaced by trouble

30 30 **to trust their heels:** to run away

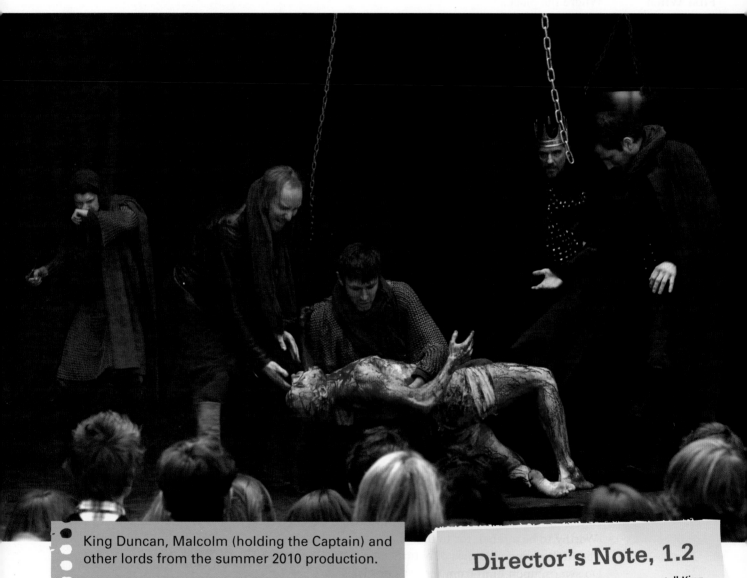

King Duncan, Malcolm (holding the Captain) and other lords from the summer 2010 production.

1 Which line(s) do you think were being spoken at the moment this picture was taken?

2 Why might Shakespeare, and the director of this production, have put so much emphasis on blood so early in the play?

3 What impact will the concentration on blood have on the audience?

Director's Note, 1.2

✔ First a wounded soldier, and then Ross, tell King Duncan that Macbeth and Banquo have won the battle.

✔ Ross also tells Duncan that the Thane of Cawdor was a traitor helping the rebels.

✔ Duncan orders Cawdor's execution, and names Macbeth the new Thane of Cawdor.

✔ Duncan sends Ross to tell Macbeth.

✔ What impression does Shakespeare give of Duncan in this scene?

	But the Norweyan lord, surveying vantage,
	With furbished arms and new supplies of men,
	Began a fresh assault.

Duncan   Dismayed not this
Our captains, Macbeth and Banquo?

Captain   Yes,
As sparrows, eagles; or the hare the lion. 35
If I say sooth, I must report they were
As cannons overcharged with double cracks,
So they doubly redoubled strokes upon the foe.
Except they meant to bathe in reeking wounds,
Or memorize another Golgotha, 40
I cannot tell.
But I am faint, my gashes cry for help.

Duncan So well thy words become thee as thy wounds;
They smack of honour both. Go get him surgeons.

Exit Captain, helped by an attendant.
Enter Ross and Angus.

  Who comes here? 45

Malcolm The worthy Thane of Ross.

Lennox What a haste looks through his eyes! So should he look
That seems to speak things strange.

Ross   God save the king.

Duncan Whence cam'st thou, worthy thane?

Ross   From Fife, great king,
Where the Norweyan banners flout the sky, 50
And fan our people cold.
Norway himself, with terrible numbers,
Assisted by that most disloyal traitor,
The Thane of Cawdor, began a dismal conflict
Till that Bellona's bridegroom, lapped in proof, 55
Confronted him with self-comparisons,
Point against point, rebellious arm 'gainst arm,
Curbing his lavish spirit. And to conclude,
The victory fell on us.

Duncan   Great happiness.

Ross That now, Sweno, the Norways' king, 60
Craves composition.
Nor would we deign him burial of his men
Till he disbursèd, at Saint Colme's Inch,
Ten thousand dollars to our general use.

Duncan No more that Thane of Cawdor shall deceive 65
Our bosom interest. Go pronounce his present death,
And with his former title greet Macbeth.

Ross I'll see it done.

Duncan What he hath lost, noble Macbeth has won.

Exit all.

31 Norweyan lord: Sweno, King of Norway
31 surveying vantage: seeing his chance
32 furbished arms: freshly cleaned weapons
36 say sooth: speak the truth
37 over-charged with double cracks: overloaded with two charges of gunpowder
39 Except: whether
39 reeking: steaming
40 memorize another Golgotha: make the battle as long-remembered as the 'the place of skulls', where Jesus was crucified
44 They smack of honour: They show you are honourable
46-7 What a haste ... things strange: He looks like someone in a hurry to give important news
49 Whence: from where
50-1 flout the sky ... our people cold: fly insultingly and fill our people with fear
54 dismal: ominous (as if Sweno would win)
55 Bellona's bridegroom ... proof: Macbeth, in strong armour, like the bridegroom of Bellona (goddess of war)
56 self-comparisons: equal skill and courage
58 Curbing: controlling
58 lavish: wild
61 Craves composition: asks to make peace
62 deign: allow
63 disbursèd: paid
63 Saint Colme's Inch: Incholm Island
64 dollars: silver coins
66 bosom interest: most important concerns
66 present: immediate

SHAKESPEARE'S WORLD

◇◇◇◇◇◇◇◇◇◇◇◇

Witches

King James I, ruler of England when *Macbeth* was written, believed wholeheartedly in witches. He was convinced that witches plotted to stop his wedding to Anne of Denmark. He had people arrested and tried for witchcraft. King James wrote a book about witches' powers, including their ability to create storms. It explained how to tell the difference between natural storms and those made by witches. It was one of many books written at the time about the powers of witches. People also wrote books challenging these ideas. However, many ordinary people shared King James' beliefs, particularly in rural communities. Witches were blamed for bad harvests, bad weather and disease (among humans and animals).

Witches were popular on the stage early in James's reign, and *Macbeth* is one of many plays they appear in. Shakespeare's witches speak in a stylised way Shakespeare sometimes uses to show a character has magical powers. Called *rhyming trochaic tetrameter*, each line has four pairs of a long syllable followed by a short one.

"I'll do, I'll do, and I'll do." (line 11), the Witches, summer 2010.

1 What impact would you expect this staging to have on the audience?
2 Do you think it is the sort of effect Shakespeare wanted?

l–r Simone Kirby, Janet Fullerlove, Karen Anderson

Actor's view

Rachel Winters
Third Witch, spring 2010

With the couplets, specifically, there's a real sense of togetherness. The Witches are one. They're doing the same thing, they've all got the same goal, they are doing it together. The rhythm of the language is so different from the rest of the language in the play, which really separates them from the other characters.

Thunder. Enter the three Witches.

First Witch   Where hast thou been, sister?

Second Witch   Killing swine.

2 **swine:** pigs

Third Witch   Sister, where thou?

First Witch   A sailor's wife had chestnuts in her lap,
And munched, and munched, and munched.   5
'Give me,' quoth I.
'Aroint thee, witch,' the rump-fed runnion cries.
Her husband's to Aleppo gone, master o' the Tiger.
But in a sieve I'll thither sail,
And, like a rat without a tail,   10
I'll do, I'll do, and I'll do.

6 **quoth:** said
7 **Aroint thee:** go away
7 **rump-fed runnion:** fat, greedy woman
8 **master:** captain
9 **thither sail:** sail there
10 **like:** disguised as
11 **I'll do:** I'll work magic on him; also suggests she'll have sex with him

Second Witch   I'll give thee a wind.

First Witch   Th' art kind.

Third Witch   And I another.

First Witch   I myself have all the other.   15
And the very ports they blow,
All the quarters that they know
I' the shipman's card.
I'll drain him dry as hay.
Sleep shall neither night nor day   20
Hang upon his pent-house lid.
He shall live a man forbid.
Weary sev'n-nights nine times nine
Shall he dwindle, peak, and pine.
Though his bark cannot be lost,   25
Yet it shall be tempest-tossed.
Look what I have.

15 **have all the other:** control the other winds
16 **ports they blow:** wind blowing from a port stops a ship landing, so the Witch can use the winds to keep the ship at sea
17–8 **quarters that … shipman's card:** compass points on a sailor's navigation chart
19 **drain him dry:** exhaust him; possibly sexually
21 **pent-house lid:** eyelid
22 **forbid:** cursed
24 **dwindle, peak, and pine:** waste away, starve
25 **bark:** ship

Second Witch   Show me, show me.

First Witch   Here I have a pilot's thumb,
Wrecked, as homeward he did come.   30

29 **pilot:** person who guides a ship into a harbour

Drums offstage.

Third Witch   A drum, a drum!
Macbeth doth come.

All Witches   The weird sisters, hand in hand,
Posters of the sea and land,
Thus do go, about, about,   35
Thrice to thine, and thrice to mine,
And thrice again, to make up nine.
Peace, the charm's wound up.

33 **weird sisters:** the Witches
34 **Posters:** fast travellers
36 **thrice:** three times
38 **Peace, the charm's wound up:** hush, be still, the spell's ready
38 **foul and fair:** refers to the bad weather (foul) and the victory (fair); it echoes the Witches in Act 1 Scene 1

Enter Macbeth and Banquo.

Macbeth   So foul and fair a day I have not seen.

Banquo   How far is't called to Forres? – What are these   40
So withered and so wild in their attire,
That look not like th' inhabitants o' th' earth,

40 **is't called:** is it supposed to be

13

Macbeth, Banquo and the Third Witch, summer 2010 production.

The Third Witch is speaking. Which of her lines do you think she is saying? Give reasons for your answer (including a quotation).

l–r Elliot Cowan, Christian Bradley, Karen Anderson

SHAKESPEARE'S WORLD

◇◇◇◇◇◇◇◇◇◇◇

Equivocation

In Elizabethan and Jacobean England, Protestantism was the only legal religion. Catholics were fined for not going to (Protestant) Church of England services, and to be a Catholic priest, or to hide one, was to be guilty of treason, punishable by death. Since 1580, Jesuit priests had secretly operated in England. They developed the doctrine of *equivocation* – that Catholics could say one thing but secretly mean another. In effect, they could lie, even on oath, to protect their priests and their fellow Catholics. In 1605, Catholic plotters failed in an attempt to blow up the King and Parliament (see page 32). Their use of equivocation during the investigation and trials was big news when Shakespeare was writing *Macbeth*.

exam SKILLS

Target skill: exploring the structural significance of a key scene

Question: How does Shakespeare present the contrast between the reactions of Banquo and Macbeth in lines 48–90?

- This scene opens with just the Witches on stage, reminding the audience of the startling opening scene.
- Rhyming lines, shorter than the blank verse used by Shakespeare for other characters, remind the audience that these creatures do not speak or behave like normal people.
- Their exchange suggests that they can torment human beings (as they do the sea captain) but not kill them.
- We soon learn that one of the Witches' techniques will be equivocation: their words to Banquo and Macbeth are ambiguous, leaving open the possibility of different interpretations.
- Because the predictions set up the tension between Macbeth and Banquo and ignite Macbeth's ambition, they are vital to the structure of the play.

- In groups of five, decide who will read each of the five parts and prepare a dramatic reading of lines 48–70. The Witches start to circle slowly round Macbeth and Banquo, who have their backs to each other as in a battle, but remain trapped in the middle.

1 What did the Macbeth and Banquo readers notice about what the Witches said to them? How did they feel when they heard lines 65–70? What did they think these lines meant? Who thought they heard the better news, Macbeth or Banquo?

2 What differences did the Witches readers notice between the reactions of Macbeth and Banquo?

3 Shakespeare's audience would have known that in the Greek and Roman world, oracles (who predicted the future) usually made ambiguous prophecies. They also knew about the doctrine of equivocation. What might they have thought about the Witches' predictions?

4 How might a modern audience's reactions to this scene differ from those of a Jacobean audience?

And yet are on't? – Live you, or are you aught
That man may question? You seem to understand me,
By each at once her choppy finger laying   45
Upon her skinny lips. You should be women,
And yet your beards forbid me to interpret
That you are so.

Macbeth   Speak, if you can. What are you?

First Witch   All hail Macbeth, hail to thee Thane of Glamis!

Second Witch   All hail Macbeth, hail to thee Thane of Cawdor!   50

Third Witch   All hail Macbeth, that shalt be king hereafter!

Banquo   Good sir, why do you start, and seem to fear
Things that do sound so fair? – I' th' name of truth,
Are ye fantastical, or that indeed
Which outwardly ye show? My noble partner   55
You greet with present grace and great prediction
Of noble having and of royal hope,
That he seems rapt withal. To me you speak not.
If you can look into the seeds of time,
And say which grain will grow, and which will not,   60
Speak then to me, who neither beg nor fear
Your favours nor your hate.

First Witch   Hail!

Second Witch   Hail!

Third Witch   Hail!   65

First Witch   Lesser than Macbeth, and greater.

Second Witch   Not so happy, yet much happier.

Third Witch   Thou shalt get kings, though thou be none.
So all hail Macbeth and Banquo!

First Witch   Banquo and Macbeth, all hail!   70

Macbeth   Stay, you imperfect speakers, tell me more.
By Sinel's death I know I am Thane of Glamis,
But how of Cawdor? The Thane of Cawdor lives,
A prosperous gentleman. And to be king
Stands not within the prospect of belief,   75
No more than to be Cawdor. Say from whence
You owe this strange intelligence, or why
Upon this blasted heath you stop our way
With such prophetic greeting?
Speak, I charge you.   *The Witches vanish.* 80

Banquo   The earth hath bubbles, as the water has,
And these are of them. Whither are they vanished?

Macbeth   Into the air: and what seemed corporal,
Melted, as breath into the wind.
Would they had stayed.   85

Banquo   Were such things here, as we do speak about?
Or have we eaten on the insane root
That takes the reason prisoner?

---

43 **aught:** anything

45 **choppy:** chapped – with dry, cracked skin
46 **should be:** appear to be

51 **hereafter:** in the future

52 **start:** jump, look shocked

54 **fantastical:** imaginary

56 **present grace:** the honour he has (Thane of Glamis)
57 **Of noble having and of royal hope:** the honour he will get (Thane of Cawdor) and becoming king in the future
58 **rapt withal:** amazed by it all, in a trance

68 **get:** be the father of

71 **imperfect:** unclear, ambiguous
72 **Sinel:** Macbeth's father

75–6 **Stands not ... belief, No more:** is no more likely

77 **intelligence:** information
78 **blasted:** barren, nothing growing there

80 **charge:** order

83 **corporal:** solid, flesh and blood

85 **Would:** I wish
87–8 **eaten on the insane root ... prisoner?:** eaten the root of the plant that sends you mad?

WHERE IS MACBETH ON THE LINE?

In line 108 the Witches' prophecies begin to come true. In this activity you have to decide **at this point in the play**, *how likely it is that Macbeth will kill the king to make another prophecy come true?*

- Read to the end of the scene. At the end of the scene how likely is it that Macbeth will kill the king?
- Base your answer only on the things Macbeth or others say.
- Imagine a line drawn across your classroom. One end represents that Macbeth is 100% likely and the other end that he is 0% likely to kill the king.
- Stand at the place on the line that corresponds with your view of how likely Macbeth is to kill the king at this point in the play.
- As a class, discuss why you are each standing where you are. Support your point with quotations from the text.

1 Now record your answer. Draw the line, mark your own position and percentage, and those of the majority of the class.

2 Find and note down quotations from the text to support your view.

3 Discuss what differences there might be between:

   a) Shakespeare's original audience

   b) a modern Globe audience in their feelings towards Macbeth at this point in the play.

4 Talk about the decisions a director could make in terms of language and stage action to influence an audience's reaction to Macbeth at this stage in the play.

exam SKILLS

Target skill: exploring the impact of key images

Question:

How does your impression of Macbeth during scene 3 compare with what you heard about him in scene 2?

One of the most effective ways in which Shakespeare works on the mind of his audience is through imagery: the pictures (images) that form in our heads when we hear particular words and strings of related words. For example, the Captain speaks of Macbeth's sword "smoking with bloody execution" and being used to kill Cawdor ("unseam'd him from the nave to the chops"). The audience's impression of Macbeth, before they see him, is therefore one of valour, which is admirable, but also of brutal violence, and this is not accidental on Shakespeare's part.

- Read Act 1 Scene 2 lines 7–41; Act 1 Scene 3 lines 48–55 and 92–109. Select from the extracts an important word or phrase that describes the character of Macbeth.
- Think of a physical action or gesture that fits with your word or phrase.
- As a group, stand in two straight lines with an aisle about a metre wide between them. Everyone should be standing opposite someone else.

- At the same time, everyone should call out their word/ phrase with their action.
- Keep repeating your word/phrase with the action over and over again as each person takes their turn to walk down the aisle in character as Macbeth.
- As you walk down the aisle, listen to the words/ phrases and think about how it feels to walk down the *Walk of Fame*.
- When you reach the end of the aisle, re-join the end of the line and continue calling out your word/phrase at the people walking down the *Walk of Fame*.

1 How did it feel to walk down the *Walk of Fame*?

2 How do you think Macbeth may have felt when he returned from the battle?

3 With a partner, choose the three quotations that give you the most striking images of Macbeth as a warrior. What gives those images their power?

4 Would an audience in Shakespeare's time have responded to the images you chose in a similar way to a modern audience?

5 Using your insights from this activity, how would you answer the question above?

Macbeth	Your children shall be kings.
Banquo	You shall be king.
Macbeth	And Thane of Cawdor too. Went it not so? 90
Banquo	To th' selfsame tune and words. — Who's here?

Enter Ross and Angus.

Ross The king hath happily received, Macbeth,
The news of thy success. And when he reads
Thy personal venture in the rebels' fight,
His wonders and his praises do contend 95
Which should be thine, or his. Silenced with that,
In viewing o'er the rest o' th' self-same day,
He finds thee in the stout Norweyan ranks,
Nothing afeard of what thyself didst make.
Strange images of death, as thick as hail 100
Came post with post, and every one did bear
Thy praises in his kingdom's great defence,
And poured them down before him.

Angus We are sent
To give thee from our royal master thanks,
Only to herald thee into his sight, 105
Not pay thee.

Ross And for an earnest of a greater honour,
He bade me, from him, call thee Thane of Cawdor:
In which addition, hail most worthy thane,
For it is thine.

Banquo What, can the devil speak true? 110

Macbeth The Thane of Cawdor lives. Why do you dress me
In borrowed robes?

Angus Who was the Thane lives yet,
But under heavy judgement bears that life
Which he deserves to lose.
Whether he was combined with those of Norway, 115
Or did line the rebel with hidden help
And vantage; or that with both he laboured
In his country's wreck, I know not.
But treasons capital, confessed and proved,
Have overthrown him.

Macbeth *[Aside.]* Glamis, and Thane of Cawdor: 120
The greatest is behind. *[To Ross and Angus.]*
Thanks for your pains.
[To Banquo.]
Do you not hope your children shall be kings,
When those that gave the Thane of Cawdor to me
Promised no less to them?

Banquo That, trusted home,
Might yet enkindle you unto the crown, 125
Besides the Thane of Cawdor. But 'tis strange:
And oftentimes, to win us to our harm,

94 **personal venture:** the risks you took and what you achieved

95-6 **His wonders ... Silenced with that:** torn between expressing his amazement and singing your praises, he's struck dumb

98 **stout:** brave

99 **Nothing afeard ... didst make:** not in the least afraid of the slaughter all around

101 **Came post with post:** were brought by messenger after messenger

105-6 **herald thee into ... pay thee:** to take you to him so he, not we, can reward you

107 **for an earnest:** as a token of honour to come

109 **addition:** extra title

113 **Who was:** He who was
113 **heavy judgement:** sentence of death
115 **combined:** allied to, working with
116 **line:** strengthen
117 **vantage:** advantages
118 **In his country's wreck:** to ruin his country
119 **treasons capital:** crimes against the state punishable by death

121 **behind:** to come

124-6 **trusted home ... the crown, Besides:** if you believe that, you might be tempted to think you'll be king as well
127-9 **to win us to our harm ... deepest consequence:** to tempt us into danger the servants of

Macbeth with other members of the cast on stage, 2001. He is saying, *Two truths are told, / As happy prologues to the swelling act* (lines 131–2).

Which other lines on the page opposite would fit with this gesture? Explain your answer.

Jasper Britton

Text Focus: Act 1 Scene 3 lines 120–150

Characters are not people: they exist only within the context of the play. As here, characters often illuminate each other: Macbeth is intrigued by the "supernatural soliciting", but Banquo thinks the witches are evil "instruments of darkness" who could "betray's in deepest consequence".

(AO1) Response to characters and events:
- Macbeth and Banquo are both heroic soldiers, but while Banquo receives only praise, Macbeth is made a thane. *Which of the two would you expect to stay loyal to his king?*
- Both characters challenge the weird sisters but have contrasting reactions to them. *Which words show how the reactions of the two characters differ?*

(AO2) Language, structure and form:
- Macbeth's real thoughts are shown only through asides. *Why does he not share his thoughts with Banquo? What difference does that make to the way an audience responds to Macbeth?*

(AO3) Context and ideas:
- Banquo suggests Macbeth might be "enkindled" to want the crown. *Why might issues of kingship have been important for Shakespeare's original audience?*

Question:
Write about the ways in which Shakespeare presents Banquo as a contrast with Macbeth in lines 120–150.

SHAKESPEARE'S WORLD

Asides

Asides are common in Shakespeare's plays. When a character speaks, and some or all of the other characters on stage can't hear, it is an aside. In this scene, Macbeth speaks to Banquo in a way that means Ross and Angus can't hear. He also speaks directly to audience, and no other character can hear. This is an important part of Shakespeare's craft as a playwright. When Macbeth speaks like this, he shares his thoughts with the audience. Usually, when this happens, the actor is alone on stage, and we call it a soliloquy. Shakespeare uses asides and soliloquies to show us what the character is really thinking. In the original Globe Theatre, as in today's, nobody in the audience was very far from the stage, and asides and soliloquies were very intimate.

Director's Note, 1.3

✔ The Witches greet Macbeth and Banquo with prophecies.
✔ Macbeth will become Thane of Glamis, and Cawdor, and then king.
✔ Banquo will be the father of a line of kings.
✔ Two nobles come from the king, calling Macbeth Thane of Glamis and Cawdor.
✔ Macbeth is distracted by the thought he might be king.
✔ How quickly does Macbeth begin thinking he may plot to become king?

The instruments of darkness tell us truths,
Win us with honest trifles, to betray's
In deepest consequence. 130
[To Ross and Angus.]   Cousins, a word, I pray you.

Macbeth *[Aside.]*   Two truths are told,
As happy prologues to the swelling act
Of the imperial theme.
[To the others.]   I thank you, gentlemen.
[Aside.]   This supernatural soliciting
Cannot be ill; cannot be good. 135
If ill, why hath it given me earnest of success
Commencing in a truth? I am Thane of Cawdor.
If good, why do I yield to that suggestion
Whose horrid image doth unfix my hair,
And make my seated heart knock at my ribs 140
Against the use of nature? Present fears
Are less than horrible imaginings.
My thought, whose murder yet is but fantastical,
Shakes so my single state of man,
That function is smothered in surmise, 145
And nothing is, but what is not.

Banquo *[To Ross and Angus.]*   Look, how our partner's rapt.

Macbeth *[Aside.]*   If chance will have me king,
Why, chance may crown me,
Without my stir. 150

Banquo *[To Ross and Angus.]*   New honours come upon him,
Like our strange garments, cleave not to their mould
But with the aid of use.

Macbeth *[Aside.]*   Come what come may,
Time and the hour runs through the roughest day.

Banquo Worthy Macbeth, we stay upon your leisure. 155

Macbeth Give me your favour.
My dull brain was wrought with things forgotten.
Kind gentlemen, your pains are registered
Where every day I turn the leaf to read them.
Let us toward the king. *[To Banquo.]* 160
Think upon what hath chanced, and at more time,
The interim having weighed it, let us speak
Our free hearts each to other.

Banquo   Very gladly.

Macbeth Till then, enough.—
Come, friends. 165

Exit all.

the Devil tell us trivial truths which, when they come true, make us believe their lies about more important matters (see *Shakespeare's World* box on page 102).
132 **happy prologues:** lucky opening (as to a play)
133 **imperial theme:** becoming king
134 **soliciting:** tempting, pressing a person to do something
136 **earnest:** token of honour to come
139 **unfix my hair:** make my hair stand on end
140 **seated:** fixed, held in place
143 **yet is but fantastical:** is just an idea
144-5 **Shakes so … smothered in surmise:** So disturbs my mind that I'm constantly thinking of it
150 **Without my stir:** without me having to do anything
152-3 **Like our strange … aid of use:** like new clothes that only fit properly when we have worn them in
153-4 **Come what … the roughest day:** Whatever happens time will pass, and even the worst day ends
155 **we stay upon your leisure:** we're waiting for you
156 **Give me your favour:** forgive me
157 **wrought with things forgotten:** tied up in thinking of what has happened
158-9 **pains are registered … to read them:** I will remember daily the help you have given me
162 **interim having weighed it:** having had time to think about it

● Macbeth and Duncan from the spring 2010 production.

In what ways do you think the actors' costumes reflect the way Shakespeare wanted to show the relationship between Macbeth and Duncan at this point?

l James Garnon, *r* Andrew Whipp

Target skill: analysing language

Question: Explore how Shakespeare presents Macbeth's ambition at this moment in the play.

Through language Shakespeare creates characters, presents dramatic events and works on our imaginations. The differences between 'public' and 'private' language are striking in this scene. Every GCSE question involves language. Think about:

- the rhythms and rhymes of Shakespearean verse
- vocabulary
- imagery and its impact
- 'voice' and tone
- who speaks to whom, and how.

For example, in Macbeth's aside in Act 1 Scene 3, he speaks of the Witches' "supernatural soliciting". You might comment that:

- because he speaks directly to the audience we hear the tension in his thoughts
- the hissing of the sibilant 's' sounds has a serpentine menace about it
- the term *supernatural* shows that he knows the witches are not human
- the word *soliciting* indicates that he knows he is being tempted.

In the next scene, Macbeth's public language is different: it gives nothing away in its artificial balance and control. Only when he reverts to the private language of his aside are his intentions made murderously plain.

In contrast, we hear Duncan speak only in public with regal confidence, addressing "sons, kinsmen, thanes", he hides nothing.

How would you answer the question above?

20

ACT 1 SCENE 4

A trumpet fanfare is played offstage. Enter Duncan, Malcolm, Donalbain, Lennox, and Attendants.

Duncan   Is execution done on Cawdor? Are not
Those in commission yet returned?

Malcolm   My liege,
They are not yet come back. But I have spoke
With one that saw him die: who did report,
That very frankly he confessed his treasons,   5
Implored your highness' pardon, and set forth
A deep repentance. Nothing in his life
Became him like the leaving it. He died
As one that had been studied in his death,
To throw away the dearest thing he owed   10
As 'twere a careless trifle.

Duncan   There's no art
To find the mind's construction in the face.
He was a gentleman on whom I built
An absolute trust.

[Enter Macbeth, Banquo, Ross and Angus.]

                                O worthiest cousin,
The sin of my ingratitude even now   15
Was heavy on me. Thou art so far before,
That swiftest wing of recompense is slow
To overtake thee. Would thou hadst less deserved,
That the proportion both of thanks and payment
Might have been mine. Only I have left to say,   20
More is thy due than more than all can pay.

Macbeth   The service and the loyalty I owe,
In doing it, pays itself. Your highness' part
Is to receive our duties. And our duties
Are to your throne and state, children and servants;   25
Which do but what they should, by doing everything
Safe toward your love and honour.

Duncan   Welcome hither.
I have begun to plant thee, and will labour
To make thee full of growing. — Noble Banquo,
That hast no less deserved, nor must be known   30
No less to have done so. Let me enfold thee,
And hold thee to my heart.

Banquo   There if I grow,
The harvest is your own.

Duncan   My plenteous joys,
Wanton in fulness, seek to hide themselves
In drops of sorrow. — Sons, kinsmen, thanes,   35
And you whose places are the nearest, know,
We will establish our estate upon
Our eldest, Malcolm; whom we name hereafter
The Prince of Cumberland. Which honour must

2 Those in commission: those sent to order the execution of Cawdor

8 Became: suited his status

9–11 been studied ... a careless trifle: has carefully chosen to throw away his life as if it was something unimportant

11–2 There's no art ... in the face: You can't work out what a person thinks and feels by just looking at them

15 The sin of my ingratitude: the fact I've not shown you my gratitude yet

16–8 Thou art so far ... overtake thee: You've done so much that it is impossible to repay you quickly enough

18 Would: if only

19–20 the proportion ... have been mine: so I could thank and repay you enough

21 More is thy due: You have earned more

24 duties: what a subject owes to a king

26–7 Which do but ... love and honour: It is our duty to do all we can to keep you safe and earn your love

30–1 nor must be ... have done so: and people must know that is so

31 enfold: embrace

34 Wanton in fulness: growing so wildly

35 drops of sorrow: tears

36 whose places are the nearest: most closely related to Duncan

39–40 Which honour ... him only: this will not be the only honour I give

SHAKESPEARE'S WORLD

◇◇◇◇◇◇◇◇◇◇◇

Succession

For Shakespeare's audience, succession – how one king or queen followed the last one – was an important political issue. From about 1590, people worried about who would succeed Queen Elizabeth. She had no children. The law was complicated, and Elizabeth refused to allow any discussion about it, so nobody was sure. When she finally died in 1603, James, already King of Scotland, was declared the next king of England.

When he became King, James chose Shakespeare and his fellow actors as his royal company – the King's Men. Perhaps this influenced Shakespeare when, about three years later, he wrote a play about Scotland and succession.

In the world of the play, though, succession is different. Duncan can choose who will be the next king. When he chooses Malcolm, Duncan makes it impossible for Macbeth to become king lawfully.

Director's Note, 1.4

✔ Duncan greets Macbeth and Banquo after the battle.
✔ Duncan announces his successor will be his son, Malcolm.
✔ Macbeth sees Malcolm is an obstacle to becoming king himself.
✔ Duncan announces he will visit Macbeth's castle, and Macbeth goes ahead to prepare.
✔ Has Macbeth decided what he is preparing for, a visit or a murder?

Lady Macbeth, 2013 production.

Both these photographs were taken before Macbeth enters (after line 52). Pick a line that might have been spoken when each photograph was taken. Why do you think the photograph fits the line?

Samantha Spiro

A

B

Not unaccompanied invest him only, 40
But signs of nobleness, like stars, shall shine
On all deservers. — From hence to Inverness,
And bind us further to you.

Macbeth The rest is labour, which is not used for you.
I'll be myself the harbinger, and make joyful 45
The hearing of my wife with your approach.
So, humbly take my leave.

Duncan   My worthy Cawdor.

Macbeth *[Aside.]* The Prince of Cumberland. That is a step
On which I must fall down, or else o'erleap,
For in my way it lies. Stars hide your fires, 50
Let not light see my black and deep desires.
The eye wink at the hand: yet let that be
Which the eye fears when it is done to see.

Exit Macbeth.

Duncan True, worthy Banquo: he is full so valiant,
And in his commendations I am fed: 55
It is a banquet to me. Let's after him,
Whose care is gone before to bid us welcome.
It is a peerless kinsman.

A fanfare of trumpets. They all exit.

ACT 1 SCENE 5

Enter Lady Macbeth, reading a letter.

Lady Macbeth *They met me in the day of success, and I have learned by
the perfect'st report, they have more in them than mortal
knowledge. When I burned in desire to question them
further, they made themselves air, into which they vanished.
Whiles I stood rapt in the wonder of it, came missives from* 5
*the king, who all-hailed me "Thane of Cawdor," by which
title, before, these weird sisters saluted me, and referred me
to the coming on of time with "Hail, king that shalt be!"
This have I thought good to deliver thee (my dearest partner
of greatness) that thou mightst not lose the dues of rejoicing* 10
*by being ignorant of what greatness is promised thee. Lay it
to thy heart, and farewell.*
Glamis thou art, and Cawdor; and shalt be
What thou art promised. Yet do I fear thy nature,
It is too full o' th' milk of human kindness 15
To catch the nearest way. Thou wouldst be great,
Art not without ambition, but without
The illness should attend it. What thou wouldst highly,
That wouldst thou holily: wouldst not play false,
And yet wouldst wrongly win. Thou'dst have, great Glamis, 20
That which cries, 'Thus thou must do,' if thou have it:
And that which rather thou do'st fear to do
Than wishest should be undone. Hie thee hither,

42 **Inverness:** where Macbeth's castle is; he intends to stay there
43 **bind us further to you:** increase our debt to you
44 **The rest ... used for you:** anything not done for you is hard work (this is for you, so it's no trouble)
45 **harbinger:** messenger who goes ahead to arrange places to stay

52–3 **The eye fears ... done to see:** Let my eye not see what my hand is doing until it is done

54 **full so:** just as brave as you say
55 **his commendations:** praises heaped upon him

58 **peerless:** without equal

2 **perfect'st:** most reliable

5 **missives:** messengers
8 **the coming on of time:** the future
9 **deliver thee:** tell you
10 **dues of rejoicing:** chance to be glad
11–2 **Lay it to thy heart:** keep it secret
15 **milk of human kindness:** compassion
16 **catch the nearest way:** take the quickest route to the crown (murder)
18 **illness should attend it:** wickedness it needs to get what it wants
18–20 **What thou would ... wrongly win:** You won't cheat to get what you want, but you don't mind winning unfairly
21 **if thou have it:** to get what you want
22–3 **that which rather ... should be undone:** you want the murder done, but fear doing it yourself

A

B

Macbeth and Lady Macbeth.

1 How would you characterise the relationship between the Macbeths in photo A?

2 How would you characterise the relationship between the Macbeths in photo B?

3 Does Shakespeare's text support both interpretations, or has one production got it wrong?

A: Elliot Cowan and Laura Rogers, summer 2010;
B: James Garnon and Claire Cox, spring 2010.

FROM THE REHEARSAL ROOM...

POWER WORDS

Act 1 Scene 5 starts with two soliloquies by Lady Macbeth (lines 13–28 and 36–52). Each member of the group is given one or more lines.

- Choose three words that seem most important in your line. These can be any words you like. For example, from line 13 you could choose *Glamis*, *Cawdor*, and *be*.

- The group reads the soliloquies out loud, each person just saying the 'power' words, not the whole line.

- Share out the images below and discuss in pairs how the images contribute to our impression of Lady Macbeth.

  - milk and human kindness

  - gold and crowns

  - hell and darkness

  - nature.

- Now read the soliloquies again. This time each person reads their whole line, giving special emphasis to the 'power' words.

1 What kind of words have people chosen?

2 What do these words tell us?

3 Comment on the impact of the imagery used by Lady Macbeth in her soliloquies.

4 This is the first time the audience meets Lady Macbeth. What first impression does Shakespeare give them of her? Explain your answer.

5 How does Lady Macbeth's view of Macbeth differ from views expressed earlier by others?

That I may pour my spirits in thine ear,
And chastise with the valour of my tongue   25
All that impedes thee from the golden round,
Which fate and metaphysical aid doth seem
To have thee crown'd withal.

Enter a Messenger.

                            What is your tidings?

Messenger   The King comes here tonight.

Lady Macbeth   Thou'rt mad to say it.
Is not thy master with him? Who, were't so,   30
Would have informed for preparation.

Messenger   So please you, it is true. Our thane is coming.
One of my fellows had the speed of him,
Who, almost dead for breath, had scarcely more
Than would make up his message.

Lady Macbeth   Give him tending,   35
He brings great news.   *Exit Messenger.*
                The raven himself is hoarse
That croaks the fatal entrance of Duncan
Under my battlements. Come you spirits
That tend on mortal thoughts, unsex me here,
And fill me from the crown to the toe, top-full   40
Of direst cruelty. Make thick my blood,
Stop up the access and passage to remorse,
That no compunctious visitings of nature
Shake my fell purpose, nor keep peace between
Th' effect and it. Come to my woman's breasts,   45
And take my milk for gall, your murd'ring ministers,
Wherever in your sightless substances
You wait on nature's mischief. Come thick night,
And pall thee in the dunnest smoke of hell,
That my keen knife see not the wound it makes,   50
Nor heaven peep through the blanket of the dark,
To cry, "Hold, hold".

Enter Macbeth.

Great Glamis, Worthy Cawdor,
Greater than both by the all-hail hereafter.
Thy letters have transported me beyond   55
This ignorant present, and I feel now
The future in the instant.

Macbeth   My dearest love,
Duncan comes here tonight.

Lady Macbeth   And when goes hence?

Macbeth   Tomorrow, as he purposes.

Lady Macbeth   O never
Shall sun that morrow see.   60
Your face, my thane, is as a book where men

---

24 **spirits:** determination
25–6 **chastise with ... golden round:** crush any argument that keeps you from taking the crown
27 **metaphysical:** supernatural

29 **tidings:** news

31 **informed for preparation:** told me so I could get everything ready
33 **had the speed:** overtook

35 **Give him tending:** Look after him

39 **tend on mortal thoughts:** listen to murderous plans
39 **unsex me:** take away my womanly nature
43 **compunctious visitings of nature:** natural feelings of pity and mercy
44 **fell:** ruthless, fierce
46 **take my milk for gall:** swap my breastmilk for a bitter juice
47 **sightless substances:** invisible shapes
48 **wait on nature's mischief:** lie in wait for humans to have evil thoughts
49 **pall:** wrap (as in a burial shroud)
49 **dunnest:** darkest

54 **all-hail hereafter:** kingship

57 **in the instant:** now

59 **as he purposes:** he plans

Target skill: analysing the presentation of a character

Question: How does Shakespeare present Lady Macbeth as a wife in Act 1 Scene 5? Refer to language, to stage action and to Shakespeare's ideas about appearance and reality.

You will be asked to write about the presentation of a character in an extract and in the play as a whole. Remember that Shakespeare presents characters through the language they use, the language used about them and through what they do on stage.

With these three things in mind, with a partner, find quotations to support or challenge the following statements about Lady Macbeth from lines 13–52.

Lady Macbeth:

1 focuses on her husband's ambition rather than her own
2 is not meant by Shakespeare to inspire the audience's sympathy
3 shows her true feelings only in her soliloquies
4 fears that although Macbeth is a valiant, violent soldier he will be afraid to commit regicide
5 knows that what she intends is unnatural and wrong
6 begs the "spirits that tend on mortal thoughts" to "unsex me here, and fill me from the crown to the toe top-full of direst cruelty" because the seventeenth century view was that women were weaker than men.
7 uses images that show she deliberately aligns herself with evil
8 seems like a witch herself
9 knows that she can dominate Macbeth.

Using your insights from this activity, how would you answer the question above?

SHAKESPEARE'S WORLD

Lady Macbeth's position in society

Women took their status in society from their husband. In the play, Macbeth was an important noble, so his wife was an important noblewoman. Women of Lady Macbeth's class managed the household. They supervised servants and managed the accounts. A large part of a woman's role was entertaining. This gave her an opportunity to demonstrate to the entire community how well she ran her household. In this scene, Lady Macbeth welcomes King Duncan into her home. Her ability to entertain guests was important to her husband's reputation and position in society. Even though these duties were important, women were always considered subordinate to men.

Duncan is greeted by Lady Macbeth, spring 2010 production.

Look at both actors when they were last on stage in this production (pages 20 and 24). What effect do the changes in costume have? Explain your answer.

Andrew Whipp and Claire Cox

May read strange matters. To beguile the time,
Look like the time: bear welcome in your eye,
Your hand, your tongue. Look like th' innocent flower,
But be the serpent under't. He that's coming   65
Must be provided for, and you shall put
This night's great business into my despatch.
Which shall to all our nights and days to come
Give solely sovereign sway and masterdom.

Macbeth   We will speak further.

Lady Macbeth   Only look up clear:
To alter favour ever is to fear.
Leave all the rest to me.

Exit Macbeth and Lady Macbeth.

ACT 1 SCENE 6

Enter servants with oboes and torches, followed by Duncan, Malcolm, Donalbain, Banquo, Lennox, Macduff, Ross, Angus, and Attendants.

Duncan   This castle hath a pleasant seat, the air
Nimbly and sweetly recommends itself
Unto our gentle senses.

Banquo   This guest of summer,
The temple-haunting martlet does approve,
By his loved mansionry, that the heaven's breath   5
Smells wooingly here. No jutty, frieze,
Buttress, nor coign of vantage, but this bird
Hath made his pendant bed and procreant cradle.
Where they most breed and haunt, I have observed
The air is delicate.   10

Enter Lady Macbeth.

Duncan   See, see, our honoured hostess.
The love that follows us sometime is our trouble,
Which still we thank as love. Herein I teach you,
How you shall bid God yield us for your pains,
And thank us for your trouble.

Lady Macbeth   All our service   15
In every point twice done, and then done double,
Were poor and single business to contend
Against those honours deep and broad wherewith
Your majesty loads our house. For those of old,
And the late dignities heaped up to them,   20
We rest your hermits.

Duncan   Where's the Thane of Cawdor?
We coursed him at the heels, and had a purpose
To be his purveyor. But he rides well,
And his great love (sharp as his spur) hath holp him
To his home before us. Fair and noble hostess   25
We are your guest tonight.

---

62 **beguile the time:** deceive people
63 **Look like the time:** behave normally
66 **provided for:** taken care of (in both meanings: feasted/murdered)
67 **despatch:** control, management
70 **Only look up clear:** Just behave normally
71 **To alter ... ever is to fear:** only fearful people keep changing their expressions

Director's Note, 1.5

✔ The letter tells us Macbeth's private thoughts, then Lady Macbeth tells us hers.
✔ Lady Macbeth worries that Macbeth will not be ruthless enough to take the crown, but she is determined to push him.
✔ News comes that Duncan will stay that night, and she decides this is the perfect time to murder him.
✔ Macbeth returns, and she tells him to leave the planning to her.
✔ Is Macbeth as committed to the plan as his wife?

1 **seat:** position, location
3 **gentle:** noble, well-born
4–5 **temple-haunting martlet ... wooingly here:** The swift (a bird), that nests in church walls, shows that the air is good by nesting here
6–7 **jutty, frieze, Buttress, nor coign of vantage:** stonework that sticks out from the main wall
8 **pendant bed and procreant cradle:** nest and cradle for its young
12–5 **The love that follows ... for your trouble:** I'm concerned by the trouble you are going to for me, but I know it is from duty and love and will reward it.
17 **single business:** feeble effort
17–8 **to contend Against:** compared to
19 **those of old:** honours you have given us in the past
20 **late dignities heaped up:** more recent ones
21 **rest your hermits:** will constantly thank you, as medieval hermits constantly pray for others
22 **coursed:** chased
22–3 **had a purpose ... his purveyor:** hoped to get here first to announce his coming

A

Macbeth, from the summer 2010 production.

Which of these two photographs do you think shows Macbeth during the soliloquy (lines 1–28)? Quote from the text to support your answer.

Elliot Cowan

Director's Note, 1.6

✔ Duncan arrives to stay at Macbeth's castle.
✔ Lady Macbeth greets him, and they exchange compliments.
✔ The audience knows that Lady Macbeth is actually planning Duncan's murder. What effect does this have on how the audience views the scene?

exam SKILLS

Target Skill: the interpretation of character

Question: Write a paragraph on what you learn about Macbeth's state of mind from the imagery in lines 1–28.

Work in pairs. One person is Macbeth's conscience, looking for reasons **not** to kill the king, while the other is his ambition, seeking reasons **to** kill Duncan.

- Hunt through Macbeth's soliloquy for verbal evidence to support your case: underline or highlight key words and images.
- Prepare a shared reading aloud of the soliloquy, deciding whether a line or words should be said by Conscience or by Ambition.
- Compare your reading with other people's versions.
- Look again through Macbeth's soliloquy and identify words relating to: murder, judgement, justice, trust, hell, heaven and ambition.

Using your insights from this activity, how would you answer the question above?

FROM THE REHEARSAL ROOM...

MACBETH ON THE LINE

This is a repeat of the activity on page 16.

- This time, do the activity and update the graph showing how likely Macbeth is to kill the king at the end of his soliloquy (line 28).

Lady Macbeth   Your servants ever
Have theirs, themselves, and what is theirs, in compt,
To make their audit at your highness' pleasure,
Still to return your own.

Duncan   Give me your hand.
Conduct me to mine host, we love him highly,   30
And shall continue our graces towards him.
By your leave, hostess.

They all exit.

ACT 1 SCENE 7

Enter servants with oboes and torches. They are followed by the Steward, and more servants carrying dishes and food. They cross the stage, and exit.

Then enter Macbeth.

Macbeth   If it were done, when 'tis done, then 'twere well
It were done quickly. If th' assassination
Could trammel up the consequence, and catch
With his surcease, success: that but this blow
Might be the be-all and the end-all. Here,   5
But here, upon this bank and shoal of time,
We'd jump the life to come. But in these cases,
We still have judgement here, that we but teach
Bloody instructions, which being taught, return
To plague th' inventor. This even-handed justice   10
Commends th' ingredients of our poisoned chalice
To our own lips. He's here in double trust:
First, as I am his kinsman, and his subject,
Strong both against the deed. Then, as his host,
Who should against his murderer shut the door,   15
Not bear the knife myself. Besides, this Duncan
Hath borne his faculties so meek, hath been
So clear in his great office, that his virtues
Will plead like angels, trumpet-tongued against
The deep damnation of his taking-off.   20
And Pity, like a naked new-born babe,
Striding the blast, or heaven's cherubin, horsed
Upon the sightless couriers of the air,
Shall blow the horrid deed in every eye,
That tears shall drown the wind. I have no spur   25
To prick the sides of my intent, but only
Vaulting ambition, which o'erleaps itself,
And falls on th' other.

Enter Lady Macbeth.

How now? What news?

Lady Macbeth   He has almost supped. Why have you left the chamber?

Macbeth   Hath he asked for me?

Lady Macbeth   Know you not he has?   30

---

27 **in compt ... highness' pleasure:** from you, in trust, always ready to return it

32 **By your leave:** Shall we go in?

1 **If it were done, when 'tis done:** (Macbeth is talking about killing Duncan)
2–4 **If th' assassination ... success:** If the murder was certain to make me king without further trouble
6 **bank and shoal of time:** in our short life on earth (compared to eternity)
7 **jump the life to come:** risk punishment in the afterlife
8–10 **that we but teach ... th' inventor:** we set others the example of violence which is then turned against us
11–2 **Commends ... our own lips:** makes us drink from our own cup of poison
12 **He's here in double trust:** he has two reasons to trust me
17–8 **borne his faculties ... great office:** has been such a good and generous king
20 **taking-off:** murder
22 **the blast:** the outcry at the murder
23 **sightless couriers of the air:** winds
25–6 **spur To prick ... my intent:** nothing to drive me to act
27 **o'erleaps:** jumps too high

29

Macbeth and Lady Macbeth, from the summer 2010 production.

The actors' body language suggests Lady Macbeth is in control at this point. What language does Shakespeare give Lady Macbeth to give this impression? Quote from the text to support your answer.

Elliot Cowan and Laura Rogers

Working cut – text for experiment

Lady M Was the hope drunk,
Wherein you dressed yourself? Hath it slept since?

Mac Pr'ythee, peace!
I dare do all that may become a man,

Lady M What beast was't, then
That made you break this enterprise to me?

Mac If we should fail?

Lady M We fail?
But screw your courage to the sticking-place,
And we'll not fail.
What cannot you and I perform upon
Th' unguarded Duncan?

Mac Bring forth men-children only,
Will it not be received,
When we have marked with blood those sleepy two
Of his own chamber, and used their very daggers,
That they have done't?

Lady M Who dares receive it other?

Mac I am settled.

YES/NO

- Get into pairs. Label yourselves **A** and **B**.

- **A**, think of something you desperately want **B** to do. It must be very important. Your job is to convince **B** to do this. However, you can only use one word to achieve your goal – "Yes".

- **B**, you do not want to do what **A** asks. You have one word to let A know – "No".

- **A** and **B**: You should both say your words in as many different ways and tones of voice as possible to persuade your partner to agree with you. Speak quietly, and concentrate on the tone of your voice not on how loud you are.

1 List the different ways you used to persuade your partner.

2 Which did you think was the most successful (and why)?

3 Compare your answers with other groups. What are the similarities and differences?

- The heart of this scene is Lady Macbeth persuading Macbeth to her point of view.

- Read the Working Cut text on the left. **A** is Lady Macbeth, **B** is Macbeth. Where it is useful, use some of the persuasion techniques you tried out in the Yes/No exercise.

4 As you answer this question, use insights you have gained from the exercise, and quotes from the text, to support your answer.

   a) How many questions are asked in this exchange, and by whom?

   b) How does Shakespeare present Lady Macbeth as a powerful and persuasive woman in this passage?

   c) How does Shakespeare present Macbeth's changing responses to Lady Macbeth during this exchange?

5 Why does Macbeth finally agree to kill his king?

6 How might a modern audience and the original Jacobean audience react differently to this scene in which Lady Macbeth persuades her husband to kill his king (regicide)?

Macbeth   We will proceed no further in this business.
He hath honoured me of late, and I have bought
Golden opinions from all sorts of people,
Which would be worn now in their newest gloss,
Not cast aside so soon.

Lady Macbeth   Was the hope drunk,
Wherein you dressed yourself? Hath it slept since?
And wakes it now, to look so green and pale
At what it did so freely? From this time,
Such I account thy love. Art thou afeard
To be the same in thine own act and valour,
As thou art in desire? Wouldst thou have that
Which thou esteem'st the ornament of life,
And live a coward in thine own esteem?
Letting "I dare not" wait upon "I would,"
Like the poor cat i' th' adage?

Macbeth   Pr'ythee, peace!
I dare do all that may become a man,
Who dares do more, is none.

Lady Macbeth   What beast was't, then
That made you break this enterprise to me?
When you durst do it, then you were a man:
And to be more than what you were, you would
Be so much more the man. Nor time, nor place
Did then adhere, and yet you would make both.
They have made themselves, and that their fitness now
Does unmake you. I have given suck, and know
How tender 'tis to love the babe that milks me —
I would, while it was smiling in my face,
Have plucked my nipple from his boneless gums,
And dashed the brains out, had I so sworn as you
Have done to this.

Macbeth   If we should fail?

Lady Macbeth   We fail?
But screw your courage to the sticking-place,
And we'll not fail. When Duncan is asleep,
(Whereto the rather shall his day's hard journey
Soundly invite him) his two chamberlains
Will I with wine and wassail so convince,
That memory, the warder of the brain,
Shall be a fume, and the receipt of reason
A limbeck only. When in swinish sleep
Their drenchéd natures lie as in a death,
What cannot you and I perform upon
Th' unguarded Duncan? What not put upon
His spongy officers, who shall bear the guilt
Of our great quell?

---

32 **of late:** recently
32-3 **bought Golden opinions:** earned a high reputation
34 **would:** should
34 **newest gloss:** while it is new
35
35-6 **Was the hope ... dressed yourself?:** Were your earlier plans made while drunk on ambition?
37 **green and pale:** hung over
39 **account:** value
40
40-1 **To be the same ... art in desire?:** to act bravely to get the thing you want
42 **the ornament of life:** the high reputation you value so much
43 **live a coward ... esteem:** live with the fact you see yourself as a coward
45 **cat i' th' adage:** the adage (proverb) is 'the cat wanted fish, but would not get her paws wet'
45 **Pr'ythee, peace!:** For heaven's sake stop pushing me!
46 **may become:** is suitable; is proper behaviour for
47 **is none:** is not a proper man
49 **durst:** dared to
50
51-2 **Nor time ... make both:** Neither the time nor the place were right then, yet you said you wished they were, so you could act
55
53-4 **They have ... unmake you:** Now the time and place *are* right, it has made you fearful of acting
54 **given suck:** breastfed a baby
58 **had I so sworn:** if I had made such a solemn promise
59 **this:** the killing of Duncan
60 **screw ... sticking place:** be brave, don't waver
60
62-3 **(Whereto ... him):** Which he's likely to do deeply after his hard journey
63 **chamberlains:** servants who put the king to bed, get him up and guard him while he sleeps
65
64 **with wine ... so convince:** get so drunk
66 **receipt of reason:** brain
67 **limbeck:** a container alcohol passes through in the distilling process
70
70 **put upon:** blame
71 **spongy officers:** the drunken servants
72 **quell:** murder

A

B

C

FROM THE REHEARSAL ROOM...

MACBETH ON THE LINE

- This is a repeat of the activity on pages 16 and 28.
- This time, do the activity and answer the questions about how likely Macbeth is to kill the king at the end of the discussion with his wife (line 83).

Director's Note, 1.7

✔ Macbeth thinks about the plan to murder Duncan, and decides not to do it.
✔ Lady Macbeth is angry at his change of plan, argues with him, and persuades him they should go ahead and murder Duncan.
✔ The balance of power shifts between Macbeth and Lady Macbeth.
✔ What are the shifts and which key lines show them?

SHAKESPEARE'S WORLD

The Gunpowder Plot

In 1605 a group of Catholic plotters (we would now call them terrorists) came up with a plan to blow up the King and both houses of Parliament, and put a Catholic on the throne. The government intelligence service found out about the plot. On the night of 4 November, they captured one of the leaders, Guy Fawkes, in a cellar under the House of Lords with enough gunpowder to blow up Parliament. Many people at the time believed kings ruled by God's will, which made a plan to kill the king even more shocking. Shakespeare wrote Macbeth a few months after the plot, and the trial of the plotters.

Macbeth and Lady Macbeth during this scene from the 2001 production.

1 Which order do you think the three photos were taken in this scene? Give reasons for your answer.
2 Pick one line from the scene to be the caption for each photo and give reasons for your answer.

Jasper Britton and Eve Best

Macbeth	Bring forth men-children only,
	For thy undaunted mettle should compose
	Nothing but males. Will it not be received,	75
	When we have marked with blood those sleepy two
	Of his own chamber, and used their very daggers,
	That they have done't?

74 undaunted mettle: fearless nature
75 received: believed

Lady Macbeth   Who dares receive it other,
As we shall make our griefs and clamour roar
Upon his death?

78 other: in any other way

Macbeth   I am settled, and bend up   80
Each corporal agent to this terrible feat.
Away, and mock the time with fairest show,
False face must hide what the false heart doth know.

80–1 I am settled … terrible feat: I'm decided and focusing my whole being on this horrible act
82 mock the time … show: behave normally to deceive everyone

Exit both.

exam PREPARATION

Text Focus: Act 1 Scene 7 lines 28–83

This is a key scene in terms of structure and of the relationship between Macbeth and Lady Macbeth. It shows Lady Macbeth's power over herself and over her husband, since if she had not goaded him into it, Macbeth might have decided to "proceed no further in this business".

(AO1) Response to characters and events:
- In this scene Macbeth is not the "Bellona's bridegroom" of earlier scenes who acts almost without thinking. *How does Shakespeare show this?*
- Most audiences, because we are given insight into his fears about the "horrid deed" of killing his king, have some sympathy for Macbeth at this point. *What are your feelings about Macbeth and Lady Macbeth at this point in the play?*
- In lines 38–52 Lady Macbeth accuses Macbeth of being a coward and less than a man. *Which of her taunts do you think hurts him most? Explain your choice.*
- Lady Macbeth is the dominant figure, showing none of Macbeth's indecision. *What finally makes Macbeth change his mind?*

(AO2) Language, structure and form:
- Shakespeare deliberately showed Macbeth as a warrior before showing him as a worrier. *Why might he have done that?*

- Macbeth is now fearful of losing his reputation, of breaking the laws of loyalty and hospitality and of "deep damnation" in "the life to come". *Which images give the most telling insight into his fears?*
- Macbeth says so little and Lady Macbeth says so much during this scene. *Why might Shakespeare have written the scene in this way?*
- *What words do Lady Macbeth and Macbeth use to refer to killing the king, and why is 'murder' not one of them?*

(AO3) Context and ideas:
- Lady Macbeth declares that she would have plucked her nipple from the boneless gums of her child "and dashed the brains out, had I so sworn as you have done to this." *How does this make you feel about Lady Macbeth? Do you think there would be a difference between the effect these lines have on modern audiences, and audiences in Shakespeare's time?*
- In the kingdom of James I unity and stability were fragile, and Guy Fawkes was recently executed when the play was first performed. *Why might this have made killing a king seem more terrible to Shakespeare's original audience?*

Question:
How is the relationship between Macbeth and Lady Macbeth presented *in this scene? Include evidence from the text to justify your view.*

Banquo, Fleance and Macbeth in the summer 2010 production.

1 What is happening on stage?

2 Why might the director have chosen to stage the scene like this?

l–r Christian Bradley, James Beesley, Elliot Cowan

FROM THE REHEARSAL ROOM...

WHAT I SAY AND WHAT I THINK

- In pairs, read lines 23–38. One read Banquo, and the other Macbeth.
- After you have read your lines, say in your own words what you think your character is really thinking. Is it the same as what you just read?

1 What does this activity tell you about Banquo and Macbeth, and their relationship at this point in the play?

SHAKESPEARE'S WORLD

Stage directions in the text

Shakespeare often suggests what actors could do in the lines the characters speak. When Banquo says, "Hold, take my sword", it is clear he is offering his sword to Fleance. However, what does Banquo offer to Fleance when he says, "Take thee that too"? In the Globe in 1606, actors could ask Shakespeare what he meant. Today, it is up to directors and actors. Some choose Banquo's cloak, others choose the diamond he has to give to Lady Macbeth (see line 17). You will find plenty more examples as you read on.

Enter Fleance carrying a torch, followed by Banquo.

Banquo	How goes the night, boy?
Fleance	The moon is down, I have not heard the clock.
Banquo	And she goes down at twelve.
Fleance	I take't 'tis later, sir.
Banquo	Hold, take my sword. 5
	There's husbandry in heaven,
	Their candles are all out. Take thee that too.
	A heavy summons lies like lead upon me,
	And yet I would not sleep.
	Merciful powers, restrain in me the cursed thoughts
	that nature 10
	Gives way to in repose.

Enter a servant carrying a torch, and Macbeth.

	Give me my sword. Who's there?
Macbeth	A friend.
Banquo	What sir, not yet at rest? The king's abed.
	He hath been in unusual pleasure, and 15
	Sent forth great largess to your offices.

Giving Macbeth a diamond.

	This diamond he greets your wife withal,
	By the name of most kind hostess, and shut up
	In measureless content.
Macbeth	Being unprepared, 20
	Our will became the servant to defect,
	Which else should free have wrought.
Banquo	All's well.
	I dreamt last night of the three weird sisters.
	To you they have showed some truth. 25
Macbeth	I think not of them.
	Yet, when we can entreat an hour to serve,
	We would spend it in some words upon that business,
	If you would grant the time.
Banquo	At your kind'st leisure. 30
Macbeth	If you shall cleave to my consent, when 'tis,
	It shall make honour for you.
Banquo	So I lose none
	In seeking to augment it, but still keep
	My bosom franchised, and allegiance clear, 35
	I shall be counselled.
Macbeth	Good repose the while.
Banquo	Thanks, sir. The like to you.

Exit Banquo and Fleance.

2 **down:** set

6 **husbandry:** careful housekeeping
7 **candles:** stars
8-9 **A heavy summons ... not sleep:** my body is begging me to sleep, but I don't want to
10-1 **nature Gives way to in repose:** come to mind when I rest

15-6 **He hath ... your offices:** He's enjoyed himself hugely and sent the servants money as a reward

18 **shut up:** gone to bed

20-2 **Being unprepared ... have wrought:** The suddenness of his arrival meant we could not do as much as we would have liked

27 **entreat an hour to serve:** can make some time
30 **At your kind'st leisure:** When it suits you
31 **shall cleave ...when 'tis:** will follow my advice when we do talk
33-4 **So I lose ... augment it:** As long as I don't have to do something dishonourable to get the honours you promise
35 **My bosom ... allegiance clear:** my conscience and duty to the king
36 **I shall be counselled:** I'll take your advice
37 **Good repose the while:** Sleep well!

Macbeth and the three Witches during Macbeth's soliloquy, summer 2010.

Shakespeare does not have a stage direction for the Witches to come on in this scene. What effect would having them so clearly linked to the dagger have on the audience's thoughts about their relationship with Macbeth? Give reasons for your answer.

Elliot Cowan, Janet Fullerlove, Simone Kirby, Karen Anderson

exam SKILLS

Target skill: analysing language

- The first half of Macbeth's speech in lines 41–72 is full of images of seeing, but after he says "it is the bloody business informs thus to mine eyes", the images are usually those of sound.
- Dramatically it is very powerful when a bell breaks the near-silence.

1 This passage starts with a lot of questions – three in the first seven lines. Why might Shakespeare have started with so many questions?

2 Always think about the images Shakespeare uses. List as many as you can in two groups – **sight** and **sound**.

3 Alliteration is another feature to look out for. What is the impact of the alliteration in lines 57–62 : "world ...wicked ...Witchcraft ...withered ...wolf...watch?"

4 Look at the structure of the sentences. Here Shakespeare wrote long sentences, then a very short one – "I go and it is done." What effect will this have on an audience?

5 You have looked at Shakespeare's use of questions, images, alliteration, and their effect on the audience. Three of these are things you should think about for any passage – which three?

Director's Note, 2.1

✔ Banquo and Macbeth meet. They are no longer easy with each other. Banquo speaks about the Witches' prophecies.

✔ Macbeth pretends to have forgotten them, but then seems to ask for Banquo's support.

✔ Banquo makes it clear he will always be loyal to Duncan.

✔ Left alone, Macbeth imagines he sees a dagger leading him to Duncan's room.

✔ What impression of Macbeth's mental state does Shakespeare create by the vision of the dagger?

Macbeth   Go bid thy mistress, when my drink is ready,
She strike upon the bell. Get thee to bed.   40

Exit Servant.

Is this a dagger which I see before me,
The handle toward my hand? Come, let me clutch thee.
I have thee not, and yet I see thee still.
Art thou not, fatal vision, sensible
To feeling as to sight? Or art thou but   45
A dagger of the mind, a false creation,
Proceeding from the heat-oppressèd brain?
I see thee yet, in form as palpable
As this which now I draw.   *[Drawing his dagger.]*
Thou marshall'st me the way that I was going,   50
And such an instrument I was to use.
Mine eyes are made the fools o' th' other senses,
Or else worth all the rest. I see thee still;
And on thy blade and dudgeon gouts of blood,
Which was not so before. There's no such thing.   55
It is the bloody business which informs
Thus to mine eyes. Now o'er the one-half world
Nature seems dead, and wicked dreams abuse
The curtained sleep. Witchcraft celebrates
Pale Hecate's offerings: and withered murder,   60
Alarumed by his sentinel, the wolf,
Whose howl's his watch, thus with his stealthy pace,
With Tarquin's ravishing strides, towards his design
Moves like a ghost. Thou sure and firm-set earth,
Hear not my steps, which way they walk, for fear   65
Thy very stones prate of my whereabout,
And take the present horror from the time,
Which now suits with it. Whiles I threat, he lives:
Words to the heat of deeds too cold breath gives.

A bell rings.

I go, and it is done. The bell invites me.   70
Hear it not, Duncan, for it is a knell,
That summons thee to heaven, or to hell.

Exit.

ACT 2 SCENE 2

Enter Lady Macbeth.

Lady Macbeth   That which hath made them drunk hath made me bold.
What hath quenched them hath given me fire.
Hark! Peace. It was the owl that shrieked,
The fatal bellman, which gives the stern'st good night. —
He is about it. The doors are open,   5
And the surfeited grooms do mock their charge
With snores. I have drugg'd their possets,
That death and nature do contend about them,
Whether they live or die.

43 **have thee not:** can't take hold of you
44–5 **sensible To feeling … sight?:** able to be touched as well as seen?
47 **heat-oppressèd:** fevered
48 **palpable:** solid, touchable
50 **marshall'st:** directs
52–3 **Mine … all the rest:** Either my eyes or my other senses are lying to me
54 **dudgeon:** handle
56–7 **bloody business … mine eyes:** thinking of murder that makes me see this
58 **abuse:** disturb
60 **Hecate:** goddess of the moon and witchcraft
61 **Alarumed:** called to act
61 **sentinel:** sentry, guard
62 **Whose howl's his watch:** who howls regularly, as a watchman calls out that all is well
63 **Tarquin:** Sextus Tarquinius, son of a Roman ruler, who raped the wife of a noble Roman (she then killed herself)
63 **ravishing:** raping
66 **prate:** tell of
67–8 **take the present … with it:** break the horrifying silence of the night, which suits my plans
68 **Whiles I threat, he lives:** While I just threaten murder, Duncan still lives
69 **Words to the heat … breath gives:** Too much talking cools the hot urge to act
71 **knell:** funeral bell

2 **quenched:** put them to sleep
4 **fatal bellman:** person who rings a bell outside the cell of a prisoner the night before he is executed
4 **stern'st:** harshest
5 **He is about it:** Macbeth's committing the murder
6–7 **surfeited … snores:** men who should be guarding Duncan are drunk and snoring
7 **possets:** hot drinks of milk mixed with alcohol
8–9 **That death … live or die:** so heavily that they may die

SHAKESPEARE'S WORLD

Regicide and Divine Right

Regicide is the legal term for the crime of killing a king.

The Reformation in the sixteenth century made some people in Europe think differently about regicide. It was normal for the king or queen to decide the religion of their country. Some extreme Protestants and Catholics began to think about killing the monarch, so that a new monarch might switch religion. There had been attempts by Catholics to assassinate both Elizabeth I and James I for this reason. Others (and James I was one of them) developed a different theory – *the divine right of kings*. This stressed that kings were put in place by God, and people had no right to challenge their monarch.

Most people in Shakespeare's original audiences would have been shocked at the idea of killing a king. Macbeth couldn't claim any higher aim – like religion – his was a crime driven by ambition.

Macbeth from the 2013 production.

1 Study the text on pages 39 and 41. When is the latest point in the scene this photo could have been taken? Give reasons for your answer.

2 What justification is there in the text for this amount of blood? Support your answer with quotations.

Joseph Millson

FROM THE REHEARSAL ROOM...

MACBETH ON THE LINE

1 Macbeth has killed the king, so he is at 100% on the graph. Look back at your graph. How decisive has Macbeth been about killing Duncan? Explain your answer

- Read what Macbeth says from line 17 to line 61.

- Is Macbeth happy with what he has done? This time give him a percentage for regret about what he did.

- Again you can stand on the line, and again the class can discuss where is the best point.

2 Now you need to record your answer. Draw the line, mark on the percentage you thought, and the general view of the class, and quote from the text to support your view.

Actor's view

Claire Cox – not killing Duncan
Lady Macbeth, spring 2010

At the time, she perhaps feels like it's a sign of weakness in herself. But it is a sign of humanity, because it's a sign that she can talk about it and tell Macbeth that he's got to do it, but when it comes to it herself, she can't really do it. She can't actually do the deed herself. To actually physically do something like that is too terrifying and there was a vulnerability about him, this older man, perhaps who really does look a bit like her father. Throughout her life she would have leant a lot on men, probably especially her father, and it would have seemed very strange to have then destroyed that. So I think it is a sign of humanity, but she feels at the time that it's a sign of weakness.

Enter Macbeth, unseen by Lady Macbeth, and carrying
two bloody daggers.

Macbeth	Who's there? What ho?	10

Lady Macbeth Alack, I am afraid they have awaked,
And 'tis not done. Th' attempt and not the deed
Confounds us. Hark! I laid their daggers ready,
He could not miss 'em. Had he not resembled
My father as he slept, I had done't.   15
My husband?

Macbeth I have done the deed.
Didst thou not hear a noise?

Lady Macbeth I heard the owl scream and the crickets cry.
Did not you speak?   20

Macbeth When?

Lady Macbeth Now.

Macbeth As I descended?

Lady Macbeth Ay.

Macbeth Hark! — Who lies i' th' second chamber?   25

Lady Macbeth Donalbain.

Macbeth This is a sorry sight.

Lady Macbeth A foolish thought, to say a sorry sight.

Macbeth There's one did laugh in's sleep,
And one cried, "Murder!" That they did wake each other.   30
I stood and heard them. But they did say their prayers,
And addressed them again to sleep.

Lady Macbeth There are two lodged together.

Macbeth One cried, "God bless us" and, "Amen" the other,
As they had seen me with these hangman's hands.   35
Listening their fear, I could not say "Amen,"
When they did say, "God bless us."

Lady Macbeth Consider it not so deeply.

Macbeth But wherefore could not I pronounce "Amen"?
I had most need of blessing, and "Amen"   40
Stuck in my throat.

Lady Macbeth   These deeds must not be thought
After these ways: so, it will make us mad.

Macbeth Methought I heard a voice cry, "Sleep no more.
Macbeth does murder sleep." The innocent sleep:
Sleep that knits up the ravelled sleeve of care,   45
The death of each day's life, sore labour's bath,
Balm of hurt minds, great nature's second course,
Chief nourisher in life's feast.

12–3 Th' attempt ... Confounds us: We'll be caught in the attempt and ruined before we can commit the deed

15 I had done't: I would have done it

27 This is a sorry sight: referring to the bloodstains on him

30 That: so

32 addressed them again to sleep: went back to sleep

33 lodged together: sleeping in the same room

35 As: as if

39 wherefore could not I pronounce: why couldn't I say

42 After: in
42 so: if we do so
45 knits up ... sleeve of care: uses knitting imagery to say that sleep calms the mind
46 sore labour's bath: the warm bath that soothes the aches of the day's work
47 balm: soothing influence on
47 great nature's second course: the main, most important, part of a meal (so the most important part of life)

A

B

Macbeth and Lady Macbeth from the summer 2010 production.

1 Which of these two photos was taken first? Give reasons for your answer.
2 Pick a line which would make a good caption for each photo, and explain your answer.

Elliot Cowan and Laura Rogers

exam SKILLS

Target skill: analysing the presentation of character through dialogue

Question: How does Shakespeare present the changing relationship between Macbeth and Lady Macbeth in lines 15–67?

- Shakespeare had Duncan murdered offstage. The audience are probably more tense because they don't see it, but wait for news with Lady Macbeth.
- Lady Macbeth's feeling that Duncan "resembled my father as he slept" will come back to haunt her.
- Sleep and death were closely linked in the minds of Jacobean audiences.

With a partner, decide whether you agree with, disagree with, or are uncertain about the statements below.

1 Lady Macbeth needed drink to get false courage.
2 Macbeth's hands are covered in blood and his mind is at breaking point.
3 The questions and very short sentences in lines 20–28 between Macbeth and Lady Macbeth reveal their nervous uncertainty.
4 Lady Macbeth is the stronger of the two since her presence of mind prevents instant discovery.

5 Macbeth's agony that he could not say "Amen" is because he knows he will be damned.
6 Thinking he heard the cry, "Sleep no more. Macbeth does murder sleep" shows that Macbeth has a conscience.
7 Saying "Consider it not so deeply" and "Who was it that thus cried?" shows that Lady Macbeth lacks imagination.
8 Because Macbeth feels overwhelmed by blood and guilt, the audience still feel sympathy for him.
9 Lady Macbeth's claim that "a little water clears us of this deed" is an example of dramatic irony.

10 Shakespeare uses the structure of this dialogue to show Lady Macbeth is the dominant partner.

Using your insights from this activity, how would you answer the question above?

Lady Macbeth	What do you mean?	
Macbeth	Still it cried, "Sleep no more" to all the house.	50
	"Glamis hath murdered sleep, and therefore Cawdor	
	Shall sleep no more. Macbeth shall sleep no more."	
Lady Macbeth	Who was it that thus cried? Why, worthy thane,	
	You do unbend your noble strength, to think	
	So brainsickly of things. Go get some water,	55
	And wash this filthy witness from your hand.	

[She sees the daggers.]

	Why did you bring these daggers from the place?	
	They must lie there. Go carry them, and smear	
	The sleepy grooms with blood.	
Macbeth	I'll go no more.	
	I am afraid to think what I have done.	60
	Look on't again, I dare not.	
Lady Macbeth	Infirm of purpose!	
	Give me the daggers. The sleeping and the dead	
	Are but as pictures. 'Tis the eye of childhood	
	That fears a painted devil. If he do bleed,	65
	I'll gild the faces of the grooms withal,	
	For it must seem their guilt.	

Exit Lady Macbeth. A loud knocking, off stage.

Macbeth	Whence is that knocking?	
	How is't with me, when every noise appals me?	
	What hands are here? Ha, they pluck out mine eyes.	70
	Will all great Neptune's ocean wash this blood	
	Clean from my hand? No. This my hand will rather	
	The multitudinous seas incarnadine,	
	Making the green one red.	

Enter Lady Macbeth, [with bloody hands].

Lady Macbeth	My hands are of your colour, but I shame	75
	To wear a heart so white. *A loud knocking, within.*	
	I hear a knocking at the south entry.	
	Retire we to our chamber.	
	A little water clears us of this deed.	
	How easy is it then! Your constancy	80
	Hath left you unattended *More loud knocking, within.*	
	Hark, more knocking:	
	Get on your nightgown, lest occasion call us	
	And show us to be watchers. — Be not lost	
	So poorly in your thoughts.	85
Macbeth	To know my deed, *More loud knocking, within.*	
	'Twere best not know myself.	
	Wake Duncan with thy knocking. I would thou couldst.	

Exit Macbeth and Lady Macbeth.

---

54 **unbend:** weaken
55 **brainsickly:** frantically, madly
56 **filthy witness:** bloody evidence of your crime
62 **Infirm of purpose!:** Weak-willed man!
64–5 **but as pictures ... painted devil:** like 'scary' pictures that only children would fear
66 **gild:** smear
66 **withal:** at the same time as leaving the daggers
67 **seem:** suggest
68 **Whence ... knocking?:** Where's that knocking coming from?

70 **What hands ... eyes:** I want to pull out my eyes so I can't see the bloodstains on my hands
71 **Neptune:** god of the sea
72–4 **This my hand ... one red:** instead, my bloodstained hands will dye the green seas red
75–6 **I shame ... so white:** I would be ashamed if I was a cowardly as you
80–1 **Your ... unattended:** your self-control has deserted you
83–4 **lest ... watchers:** in case people call us and see we have not been asleep in our beds

85 **so poorly:** in such a cowardly way

Director's Note, 2.2

✔ Lady Macbeth waits for Macbeth while he kills Duncan.
✔ Macbeth is horrified by what he has done, and he has spoilt the plan, by not leaving the daggers he used next to the grooms.
✔ Macbeth will not take the daggers back, so Lady Macbeth takes control – she does take them back.
✔ Somebody knocks at the castle gate. Lady Macbeth urges Macbeth to wash the blood off and change.
✔ Who is the dominant partner in this scene?

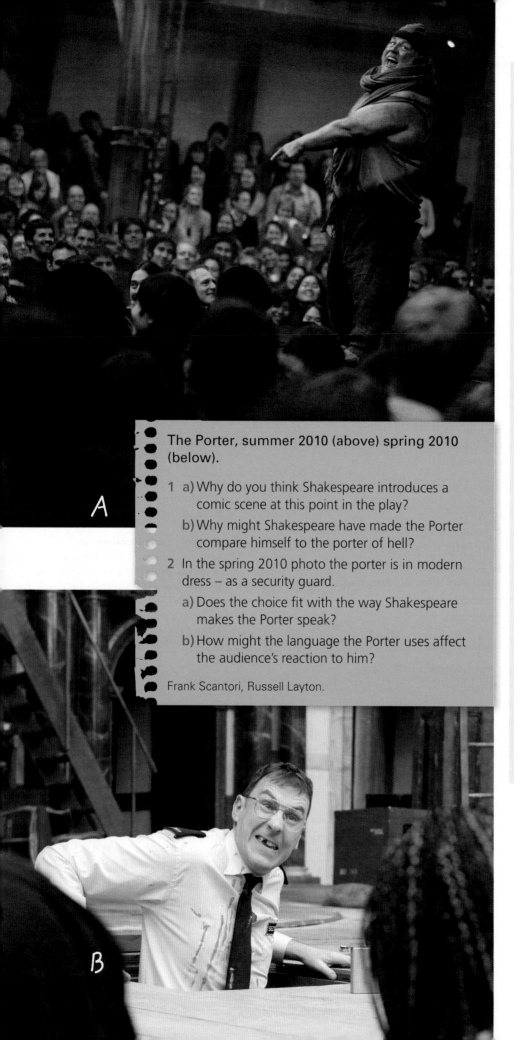

A

The Porter, summer 2010 (above) spring 2010 (below).

1 a) Why do you think Shakespeare introduces a comic scene at this point in the play?

 b) Why might Shakespeare have made the Porter compare himself to the porter of hell?

2 In the spring 2010 photo the porter is in modern dress – as a security guard.

 a) Does the choice fit with the way Shakespeare makes the Porter speak?

 b) How might the language the Porter uses affect the audience's reaction to him?

Frank Scantori, Russell Layton.

B

Director's view

Bill Buckhurst
Director, spring 2010

[At the end of the murder scene] the stage is left empty for a moment, with the audience absolutely with their hearts in their mouths, having seen this gruesomeness.

And then the Porter arrives to answer the door, and in our production he comes up through a trap, as if his office is below stairs. What happens is the audience have their hearts in their mouths and Lady Macbeth and Macbeth leave and there's a few moments as the knocking goes on, and there's this 'BANG!' of the trap opening, which gives everyone a shock … which is quite nice! And interesting to see the audience respond to that as their nerves are on edge.

I think it's a brilliantly structured bit of storytelling. Just at the moment when the audience are wrung out, strung out and have been thrown around the place by the storytelling and the tension which has been built up, on comes this guy who cracks a few jokes. It's a bit of comic relief for us to gather ourselves before the story continues.

And it works terribly well as it gives a little bit of respite after this very intense story which has been taken to a real climactic point. We almost forget about the story for a moment, and then Macduff arrives with Lennox, and we're straight back into it. Also, it gives enough time for the actor playing Macbeth to get clean! We did do a bit of research on how much blood [there would be] if you hit a major artery – there's going to be a lot of blood, it's going to be everywhere, pints and pints of blood all over him. So he had it on his shirt, on his face, on his hands, and he needs time to get changed, to get rid of the evidence, so he can come in completely calmly.

Enter a Porter.

More loud knocking within.

Porter Here's a knocking indeed. If a man were porter of hell gate, he should have old turning the key.

More loud knocking within.

Knock, knock, knock. Who's there, i' the name of Belzebub? Here's a farmer, that hanged himself on th' expectation of plenty. Come in time, have napkins enough about you, here you'll sweat for't. 5

More loud knocking off stage.

Knock, knock. Who's there in th' other devil's name? Faith, here's an equivocator, that could swear in both the scales against either scale, who committed treason enough for God's sake, yet could not equivocate to heaven. O come in, equivocator. 10

More loud knocking within.

Knock, knock, knock! Who's there? Faith, here's an English tailor come hither, for stealing out of a French hose. Come in tailor, here you may roast your goose.

More loud knocking within.

Knock, knock. Never at quiet. What are you? — But this place is too cold for hell. I'll devil-porter it no further. I had thought to have let in some of all professions that go the primrose way to the everlasting bonfire. 15

More loud knocking within.

Anon, anon! I pray you, remember the porter.

[He opens the door. Enter Macduff and Lennox.]

Macduff Was it so late, friend, ere you went to bed, 20
That you do lie so late?

Porter Faith, sir, we were carousing till the second cock, and drink, sir, is a great provoker of three things.

Macduff What three things does drink especially provoke?

Porter Marry, sir, nose-painting, sleep, and urine. Lechery, sir, 25
it provokes and unprovokes. It provokes the desire, but it takes away the performance. Therefore much drink may be said to be an equivocator with lechery. It makes him, and it mars him; it sets him on, and it takes him off; it persuades him, and disheartens him; makes him 30
stand to, and not stand to. In conclusion, equivocates him in a sleep, and giving him the lie, leaves him.

Macduff I believe drink gave thee the lie last night.

Porter That it did, sir, i' the very throat on me. But I requited him for his lie, and (I think) being too strong for him, 35
though he took up my legs sometime, yet I made a shift to cast him.

2 **have old:** plenty of

4 **Belzebub:** the devil

5 **th' expectation of plenty:** when a good harvest was predicted (so he couldn't charge as much)

5 **Come in time:** you've come at the right time

6 **napkins:** handkerchiefs (to mop up the sweat)

8 **equivocator:** someone who deliberately says things that can be understood in different ways

8–11 **that could swear ... heaven:** that could argue each side of an argument so well that the scales of Justice were balanced, but who could not talk his way into heaven

13–4 **stealing out ... hose:** French hose (cloth leggings or stockings) were wide, English ones less so. The porter is accusing the tailor of re-shaping French hose, to steal the extra fabric.

14 **roast your goose:** heat your tailor's iron (called 'goose' because of its shape)

18 **primrose way ... bonfire:** attractive-looking, sinful, path to hell

19 **remember:** remember to tip – give money for the services of

20 **ere:** before

22 **carousing till the second cock:** drinking until three in the morning

23 **is a great provoker of:** often sets off

25 **Marry:** By the Virgin Mary, used at the start of a sentence for emphasis as 'Well' can be now

25 **nose-painting:** getting a red nose (through drinking too much)

25 **Lechery:** lust, sexual desire

27–31 **It makes him ... not stand to:** the rest of the speech keeps contrasting the way drink makes a man lustful but, at the same time, unable to have sex

31–2 **In conclusion ... leaves him:** so drink deceives the drinker

34–5 **requited him:** paid him back (drink, which he is talking of as an equivocator)

36–7 **though he took ... cast him:** though he made me fall, I managed to get rid of him, by being sick (using the vocabulary of a wrestling match)

43

Macbeth (without trousers) and Macduff, 2001 production.

1 Is there any justification in the text for Macbeth being on stage without his trousers on?
2 What point in the scene is this? Give reasons for your answer. (It is on page 45.)

Jasper Britton and Liam Brennan

Director's view

Bill Buckhurst
Director, spring 2010

And what is lovely about it is that we, as the audience, know the truth that no one else on stage does, and we're interested to see how Macbeth deals with the arrival of these people – how cool he is. It all depends on how the actor plays it, but the words Macbeth has been given are very, very good and can be very amusing for an audience. Once Macduff's gone off to look for Duncan, Lennox talks about these strange things that have happened that night, almost like omens. And Macbeth just listens and he responds in a half line: "Twas a rough night." It always brings the house down – I've never seen it in this show with the audience not finding it hilarious! Talk about the understatement of the century!

So the scene then builds, as all these people arrive on stage, discovering the news of the killing. Macbeth obviously goes to the extremes by going off and killing the two grooms. He is questioned by Macduff: "Why did you do it"? And Macbeth starts talking, digging himself a grave, about why he did it. So much so, that it builds to Lady Macbeth (who we think, in rehearsals, is actually faking the faint, to distract attention away for him) and it's very exciting.

SHAKESPEARE'S WORLD
◇◇◇◇◇◇◇◇◇◇◇◇

Weather portents
People in Shakespeare's time had a collection of rhymes and phrases to predict the weather, just as we do today. They might look at the sky, rivers or at the behaviour of animals and forecast snow, sunshine or storms. Their sayings, like ours, were based on experience and evidence, as well as folklore.

Superstitious members of the Globe audience made predictions about their own lives based on the weather. Some thought thunder on Monday meant a woman would die, while thunder on Thursday promised plenty of sheep. Some thought the weather's direction showed its nature; an east wind, for example, was thought to be evil, as explained in the Bible. Earthquakes, as mentioned by Lennox in *Macbeth*, were seen as a sign of God's anger, sent to make sinners repent.

38 **stirring:** awake yet

Enter Macbeth not seen at first by Macduff.

Macduff Is thy master stirring?
Our knocking has awak'd him. Here he comes.

Lennox Good morrow, noble sir.

Macbeth Good morrow, both! 40

Macduff Is the king stirring, worthy thane?

Macbeth Not yet.

Macduff He did command me to call timely on him,
I have almost slipped the hour.

42 **timely:** early
43 **slipped:** missed

Macbeth I'll bring you to him.

Macduff I know this is a joyful trouble to you, 45
But yet 'tis one.

45-6 **this is a ... 'tis one:** you have had pleasure in the king's visit, but it is a lot of work

Macbeth The labour we delight in physics pain.
This is the door.

47 **The labour ... physics pain:** the delight we get from work we enjoy cures any pain it causes

Macduff I'll make so bold to call,
For 'tis my limited service. *Exit Macduff.*

49 **my limited service:** it is part of my job

Lennox Goes the king hence today? 50

50 **hence:** away from here

Macbeth He does. He did appoint so.

Lennox The night has been unruly.
 Where we lay, our chimneys were blown down,
And (as they say) lamentings heard i' th' air,
Strange screams of death, 55
And prophesying, with accents terrible,
Of dire combustion and confused events,
New hatched to th' woeful time.
The obscure bird clamoured the live-long night.
Some say the earth was feverous and did shake. 60

52 **unruly:** wild, stormy

56-8 **prophesying, with accents ... woeful time:** saying, in a horrible tone of voice, that something terrible (bringing confusion, chaos and misery) was about to happen
59 **obscure bird:** owl
59 **clamoured:** hooted loudly

Macbeth 'Twas a rough night.

Lennox My young remembrance cannot parallel
A fellow to it. *Enter Macduff.*

62-3 **My young ... fellow to it:** I can't remember a night this bad but then I'm young

Macduff O horror, horror, horror!
Tongue nor heart cannot conceive nor name thee. 65

65 **conceive:** think of, imagine

**Macbeth and
Lennox** What's the matter?

67 **Confusion:** Chaos
67 **masterpiece:** his most important piece of work

Macduff Confusion now hath made his masterpiece.
Most sacrilegious murder hath broke ope
The Lord's anointed temple, and stole thence
The life o' th' building. 70

68 **sacrilegious:** sin against God
68 **ope:** open
69-70 **The Lord's anointed ... th' building:** the king's body (he was seen as appointed by God) and taken his life

Macbeth What is't you say? The life?

Lennox Mean you his majesty?

Macduff Approach the chamber, and destroy your sight
With a new Gorgon. Do not bid me speak.

74 **Gorgon:** in Greek myths, a monster who turned those who looked at her to stone

45

FROM THE REHEARSAL ROOM...

LISTENING FOR THE KEY WORDS

In groups of six, read through the *Working Cut*, each taking one part.

- This is a listening activity, don't look at your script until you need to say your lines. To help you, the person reading will say the next speaker's name. So Don(albain) when you say "What is amiss?" you then say, "Macbeth".

- Each time before you say your own lines, you must repeat the most important word or phrase that the character before you has just said. Listen hard, and don't cheat by reading.

1 a) What did you notice about the important words or phrases that were chosen?

   b) Were there any patterns in the words or particular types of words that were repeated?

2 How does looking at the important words chosen for each character help us understand more about the characters and their relationships in this scene? Explain your answer.

Working Cut – text for experiment

Mac	Had I but died an hour before this chance, I had lived a blessed time. For from this instant There's nothing serious in mortality.
Don	What is amiss?
Mac	You are, and do not know't.
Duff	Your royal father's murdered.
Malc	O, by whom?
Len	Those of his chamber, as it seemed, had done't. Their hands and faces were all badged with blood.
Mac	O, yet I do repent me of my fury, That I did kill them.
Malc	Why do we hold our tongues?
Don	What should be spoken here?
Banq	Let us meet And question this most bloody piece of work To know it further.
Mac	Let's briefly put on manly readiness, And meet i' th' hall together.
Malc	What will you do? I'll to England.
Don	To Ireland, I.

See, and then speak yourselves.

Exit Macbeth and Lennox.

                        Awake, awake!   75
Ring the alarum bell. Murder and treason!
Banquo and Donalbain! Malcolm awake!
Shake off this downy sleep, death's counterfeit,
And look on death itself. Up, up, and see
The great doom's image. Malcolm, Banquo,   80
As from your graves rise up, and walk like sprites
To countenance this horror. – Ring the bell!

Bell rings. Enter Lady Macbeth.

Lady Macbeth What's the business?
That such a hideous trumpet calls to parley
The sleepers of the house? Speak, speak!   85

Macduff O gentle lady,
'Tis not for you to hear what I can speak.
The repetition, in a woman's ear,
Would murder as it fell.

Enter Banquo.

O Banquo, Banquo! Our royal master's murdered.   90

Lady Macbeth Woe, alas!
What, in our house?

Banquo   Too cruel anywhere.
Dear Duff, I pr'ythee, contradict thyself,
And say it is not so.

Enter Macbeth, Lennox and Ross.

Macbeth Had I but died an hour before this chance,   95
I had lived a blessed time. For from this instant
There's nothing serious in mortality.
All is but toys. Renown and grace is dead,
The wine of life is drawn, and the mere lees
Is left this vault to brag of.   100

Enter Malcolm and Donalbain.

Donalbain What is amiss?

Macbeth   You are, and do not know't.
The spring, the head, the fountain of your blood
Is stopped, the very source of it is stopped.

Macduff Your royal father's murdered.

Malcolm   O, by whom?

Lennox Those of his chamber, as it seemed, had done't.   105
Their hands and faces were all badged with blood,
So were their daggers, which, unwiped, we found
Upon their pillows. They stared and were distracted.
No man's life was to be trusted with them.

Macbeth O, yet I do repent me of my fury,   110

---

78 downy: soft, cosy

80 The great doom's image: a sight as horrifying as the Last Judgement (when the dead rise to be judged by Christ)
81 sprites: spirits
82 countenance: look on

84 That such ... parley: that you call everyone to you so loudly

88–9 The repetition ... as it fell: telling a woman this news would kill her

93 pr'ythee: short for 'I pray you', please

95 chance: event

97–8 serious in mortality ... toys: life and death are unimportant, everything's trivial
98 Renown and grace: honour
99–100 The wine ... brag of: The wine of life's been taken from the barrel, the cellar's empty, there's nothing left to boast of but the bitter sediment at the bottom
101 What is amiss?: What's wrong?
102 The spring ... your blood: your father
103 stopped: dead

106 badged: marked

108 distracted: confused, befuddled

Target skill: analysing a key dramatic moment

Question: How does Shakespeare present the reactions to the discovery of Duncan's murder?

Structurally, Act 2 Scene 3 lines 83–123 is important: the discovery of Duncan's body starts a crisis. The crisis ends with Macbeth as king; he has risen, and we will watch him fall.

- Regicide would appal a Jacobean audience, most of whom believed that a king's right to rule came from God.
- Although Malcolm is Duncan's designated heir, he and Donalbain flee from Scotland.
- Macduff begins to emerge as an opponent of Macbeth.
- There is a gap between what most of the characters say and what we guess they are thinking.

- Macbeth confesses to killing the grooms; his language becomes increasingly elaborate and artificial.
- Banquo declares, "In the great hand of God I stand" and speaks of "treasonous malice".
- The difference between what is apparent and what is real is a major theme in the play.

Investigate in groups of three (**A**, **B** and **C**):
- **A** looks for evidence that Lady Macbeth really does faint; **B** seeks to prove that she pretends to, in order to stop Macbeth giving too much away. **C** reviews the evidence and decides if one case is stronger.
- Compare your conclusions with others.
- If you were the director, what would you want the audience to think?

Using your insights from this activity, how would you answer the question above?

Members of the Court including Banquo (partly obscured) Malcolm (back to us) and Macbeth (white shirt), spring 2010.

Which line was being spoken when this photo was taken?
Quote directly from the text to support your answer.

	That I did kill them.
Macduff	Wherefore did you so?
Macbeth	Who can be wise, amazed, temperate, and furious,
	Loyal, and neutral, in a moment? No man.
	Th' expedition of my violent love
	Outran the pauser, reason. Here lay Duncan,
	His silver skin laced with his golden blood,
	And his gashed stabs looked like a breach in nature
	For ruin's wasteful entrance. There the murderers,
	Steeped in the colours of their trade, their daggers
	Unmannerly breeched with gore. Who could refrain,
	That had a heart to love, and in that heart
	Courage to make's love known?
Lady Macbeth	Help me hence, ho!
Macduff	Look to the Lady.

[Lady Macbeth faints, or pretends to faint. While others look after her, Malcolm and Donalbain talk.]

Malcolm	Why do we hold our tongues,
	That most may claim this argument for ours?
Donalbain	What should be spoken here,
	Where our fate hid in an auger hole,
	May rush, and seize us? Let's away,
	Our tears are not yet brewed.
Malcolm	Nor our strong sorrow upon the foot of motion.
Banquo	Look to the Lady.

[Lady Macbeth may be helped offstage.]

	And when we have our naked frailties hid,
	That suffer in exposure, let us meet
	And question this most bloody piece of work
	To know it further. Fears and scruples shake us.
	In the great hand of God I stand, and thence,
	Against the undivulged pretence, I fight
	Of treasonous malice.
Macduff	And so do I.
All	So all.
Macbeth	Let's briefly put on manly readiness,
	And meet i' th' hall together.
All	Well contented.

Exit all except Malcolm and Donalbain.

Malcolm	What will you do? Let's not consort with them.
	To show an unfelt sorrow is an office
	Which the false man does easy. I'll to England.
Donalbain	To Ireland, I. Our separated fortune
	Shall keep us both the safer. Where we are,
	There's daggers in men's smiles. The near in blood,
	The nearer bloody.

111 Wherefore: why

112 temperate: calm

114–5 Th' expedition ... pauser, reason: my love for Duncan was so great I acted without thinking
116 laced with: covered in streaks of
117–8 breach in nature ... wasteful entrance: the castle walls were broken down to let the enemy in (describing the wounds that caused Duncan's death)
119 Steeped in ... their trade: soaked in blood
120 Unmannerly breeched with gore: indecently covered in blood
122 make's: make his

125 That most ... argument for ours: letting others show the grief we have most right to (as his sons)
126–8 What should ... seize us: What can we say when we don't know who the murderer is and we may be next?

130 upon the foot of motion: ready to flow
132–3 our naked ... in exposure: dressed

135 scruples: doubts, suspicions
136–8 In the great hand ... malice: I trust God to protect me and help me fight these unknown traitors

140 briefly put on manly readiness: take a moment to quickly dress

143 consort: meet with
143 office: action
146–7 Our separated ... the safer: We'll be safer apart
148–9 The near in ... nearer bloody: As Duncan's sons we are most in danger of getting killed next

49

ACT 2 SCENE 4

Malcolm	This murderous shaft that's shot	150
	Hath not yet lighted, and our safest way	
	Is to avoid the aim. Therefore to horse,	
	And let us not be dainty of leave-taking,	
	But shift away. There's warrant in that theft	
	Which steals itself, when there's no mercy left.	155

Exit Malcolm and Donalbain.

ACT 2 SCENE 4

Enter Ross, with an old man.

Old Man   Threescore and ten I can remember well:
Within the volume of which time I have seen
Hours dreadful and things strange. But this sore night
Hath trifled former knowings.

Ross   Ha, good father,   5
Thou seest, the heavens, as troubled with man's act,
Threaten his bloody stage. By th' clock 'tis day,
And yet dark night strangles the travelling lamp.
Is't night's predominance, or the day's shame,
That darkness does the face of earth entomb,   10
When living light should kiss it?

Old Man   'Tis unnatural,
Even like the deed that's done. On Tuesday last,
A falcon, towering in her pride of place,
Was by a mousing owl hawked at and killed.   15

Ross   And Duncan's horses, (a thing most strange and certain)
Beauteous and swift, the minions of their race,
Turned wild in nature, broke their stalls, flung out,
Contending 'gainst obedience, as they would
Make war with mankind.   20

Old Man   'Tis said they ate each other.

Ross   They did so, to th' amazement of mine eyes
That looked upon't.

Enter Macduff.

Here comes the good Macduff.
How goes the world, sir, now?

Macduff   Why, see you not?

Ross   Is't known who did this more than bloody deed?   25

Macduff   Those that Macbeth hath slain.

Ross   Alas, the day!
What good could they pretend?

Macduff   They were suborned.
Malcolm and Donalbain, the king's two sons,
Are stol'n away and fled, which puts upon them
Suspicion of the deed.

150-2 This murderous ... avoid the aim: Let's leave, before we become the targets

153 dainty of leave-taking: concerned to say goodbye properly

154-5 There's warrant ... no mercy left: stealing away is justified under the circumstances

Director's Note, 2.3

✔ A drunken Porter lets in Macduff and Lennox to wake up Duncan.
✔ Macbeth joins them, while Macduff goes to wake Duncan.
✔ Macduff returns with the news Duncan is dead.
✔ Macbeth and Lennox go to see. When they return Lennox says the guards did it, and Macbeth says he killed them.
✔ Why do Duncan's sons decide to flee abroad?

1 Threescore and ten: seventy years
2 volume: space
3 sore: bitter, painful
4 Hath trifled former knowings: they are nothing compared to this
6-7 as troubled ... bloody stage: disturbed by what has happened, threaten the earth
8 travelling lamp: the sun
9-11 Is't night's ... kiss it?: Is it so dark because night is more powerful, or because the day is too ashamed to show its face?
14 towering in her pride of place: at the highest point of her flight
15 a mousing owl: an owl that usually lives off mice (owls would not normally attack a falcon)
17 minions of their race: most elegant of their kind
19 Contending 'gainst obedience: rebelling against their training
19 as: as if
27 What good could they pretend?: What benefit could they expect to gain by it?
27 suborned: bribed

Ross	'Gainst nature still.	30
	Thriftless ambition, that wilt ravin up	
	Thine own life's means. Then 'tis most like	
	The sovereignty will fall upon Macbeth.	
Macduff	He is already named; and gone to Scone	
	To be invested.	35
Ross	Where is Duncan's body?	
Macduff	Carried to Colmekill,	
	The sacred storehouse of his predecessors,	
	And guardian of their bones.	
Ross	Will you to Scone?	
Macduff	No cousin, I'll to Fife.	40
Ross	Well, I will thither	
Macduff	Well, may you see things well done there. Adieu,	
	Lest our old robes sit easier than our new.	
Ross	Farewell, father.	
Old Man	God's benison go with you, and with those	45
	That would make good of bad, and friends of foes.	

Exit all.

30–2 **'Gainst nature ... life's means:** Another unnatural act – devouring the body that gave them life

32 **like:** likely

34 **Scone:** where Scottish kings were crowned

35 **invested:** crowned

37 **Colmekill:** the island where Scottish kings were buried

41 **thither:** there (to Scone)

43 **Lest our old ... our new:** It is possible that our new situation will be worse than the old one (using clothing imagery)

45 **benison:** blessing

exam SKILLS

Target skill: interpreting images

Question: How does Shakespeare use imagery to portray Scotland in Act 2 Scene 4 lines 1–35?

- The play *Macbeth* (like most of Shakespeare's tragedies) focuses on great, royal or noble people, but this scene, which brings in an ordinary person, is a commentary on the impact of regicide.
- The night of Duncan's murder was "unruly" – there were "lamentings heard i'th'air" and "Strange screams of death." The Old Man has "seen hours dreadful and things strange" but thinks that "this sore night hath trifled former knowings."
- Macduff's words later in the scene are full of bitter irony.
- Macduff's line, "Lest our old robes sit easier than our new" is one of several clothing images in the play. Along with his absence from the coronation, it reinforces Macduff's hostility to Macbeth.

1 Find images from lines 1–22 which refer to: light and dark; theatre; time; birds; animals.
2 Choose three of the images and explain how Shakespeare uses each of them to build a picture of Scotland after Duncan's murder.
3 What cumulative effect would you expect these images to have on modern audiences?
4 Using your insights from this activity, answer the question above.

Director's Note, 2.4

✔ Ross and an old man discuss unnatural happenings, which suggest evil times.
✔ Macduff joins them, bringing the news that because Malcolm and Donalbain have fled, they are blamed for Duncan's murder.
✔ Macbeth has been chosen king.
✔ What difference is there in Ross' and Macduff's reaction to the news that Macbeth is the new king?

ACT 3 SCENE 1

Enter Banquo.

Banquo   Thou hast it now, king, Cawdor, Glamis, all,
As the weird women promised, and, I fear,
Thou play'dst most foully for't. Yet it was said
It should not stand in thy posterity,
But that myself should be the root and father   5
Of many kings. If there come truth from them,
As upon thee Macbeth, their speeches shine,
Why, by the verities on thee made good,
May they not be my oracles as well,
And set me up in hope? But hush, no more.   10

3 **play'dst most foully for't:** acted evilly to get it
4 **It should not ... posterity:** your sons would not be king
6 **them:** the Witches
8 **verities on thee made good:** promises that have come true for you
9 **oracles:** predictors of the future

exam SKILLS

Target skill: analysis of character and context

- In Shakespeare's source, Holinshed's *Chronicles*, Banquo was Macbeth's accomplice rather than a more honourable contrast to him.

1 What does Banquo think about Macbeth, and about the Witches' prophecies?
2 What advantages might Shakespeare have seen in making his Banquo different from the one who was Macbeth's accomplice in his source?

'Enter Macbeth as King, Lady Macbeth as Queen,' spring 2010.

1 What has the director done to show Macbeth's new royal status?
2 Explain, with quotations from page 53, how Shakespeare showed Macbeth's new status.

Claire Cox and James Garnon

A trumpet call is played.
Enter Macbeth as King, Lady Macbeth as Queen,
Lennox, Ross, Lords and Attendants.

Macbeth   Here's our chief guest.

Lady Macbeth   If he had been forgotten,
It had been as a gap in our great feast,
And all-thing unbecoming.

Macbeth   Tonight we hold a solemn supper, sir,   15
And I'll request your presence.

Banquo   Let your highness
Command upon me, to the which my duties
Are with a most indissoluble tie
For ever knit.   20

Macbeth   Ride you this afternoon?

Banquo   Ay, my good lord.

Macbeth   We should have else desired your good advice
(Which still hath been both grave and prosperous)
In this day's council. But we'll talk tomorrow.
Is't far you ride?   25

Banquo   As far, my lord, as will fill up the time
'Twixt this and supper. Go not my horse the better,
I must become a borrower of the night,
For a dark hour or twain.

Macbeth   Fail not our feast.

Banquo   My lord, I will not.   30

Macbeth   We hear our bloody cousins are bestowed
In England and in Ireland, not confessing
Their cruel parricide, filling their hearers
With strange invention. But of that tomorrow;
When therewithal, we shall have cause of state   35
Craving us jointly. Hie you to horse.
Adieu, till you return at night.
Goes Fleance with you?

Banquo   Ay, my good lord. Our time does call upon's.

Macbeth   I wish your horses swift and sure of foot.   40
And so I do commend you to their backs.
Farewell.   *Exit Banquo.*
Let every man be master of his time
Till seven at night, to make society
The sweeter welcome.   45
We will keep ourself till supper time alone.
While then, God be with you!

Exit all but Macbeth and a Servant.

Sirrah, a word with you. Attend those men
Our pleasure?

Servant   They are, my lord, without the palace gate.   50

14 **all-thing:** completely

19-20 **with a most ... knit:** tied with an unbreakable knot

22 **else:** otherwise

23 **Which still ... and prosperous:** Which has always been carefully considered and useful
24 **this day's council:** today's meeting with my advisors

27-9 **Go not my horse ... twain:** even now, no matter how fast I ride, it will be dark for an hour or two before I get back

31 **bloody cousins:** Malcolm and Donalbain ('bloody' to remind people that they are said to have killed Duncan)
33 **parricide:** killing of their father
34 **strange invention:** unbelievable lies
35-6 **When therewithal ... jointly:** When we will also need to discuss matters of government
39 **Our time does call upon's:** We really must go

43 **be master of his time:** be free to do as he likes
44-5 **society The sweeter welcome:** meeting together again something to look forward to
47 **While:** until

48 **Sirrah:** You, used to call a less important person
48-9 **Attend those men Our pleasure?:** Are the men waiting?
50 **without:** outside

A

B

Macbeth during the soliloquy (lines 52–76).

1 In A how does Shakespeare's language convey the uncertainty that James Garnon is conveying with his body language?

2 Pick a line from the soliloquy which Elliot Cowan was most likely to be speaking when the photo (B) was taken. Quote from the text to support your answer.

A: James Garnon, spring 2010.
B: Elliot Cowan, summer 2010.

exam PREPARATION

Text Focus: Act 3 Scene 1 lines 50–76

This soliloquy shows us that although he is king, Macbeth is fearful, insecure and increasingly alone.

(AO1) Response to characters and events:

- Kingship has not proved to be what Macbeth had hoped – "To be thus is nothing" – he has none of the satisfaction that he killed for. *Why is this?*
- Macbeth is now king but the audience realise that his first act, which sets the tone for his reign, will be the treacherous murder of Banquo. *When he claims "there is none but he whose being I do fear", do we believe him?*
- Macbeth is positive about (jealous of?) Banquo's virtues: his "royalty of nature", the "dauntless temper of his mind" and the "wisdom that doth guide his valour to act in safety". *Why might Shakespeare have chosen to emphasise Banquo's virtues at this point?*

(AO2) Language, structure and form:

- Macbeth uses the language of royalty about Banquo ("royalty...reigns"), and compares him to the Roman ruler [Octavius] Caesar while he compares himself to Mark Antony (Octavius beat Antony in a civil war and became the Emperor Augustus.) *What do these images tell us about his state of mind?*
- His image of "mine eternal jewel" makes the soul something hard, object-like and non-human. *How has Macbeth lost any sense of being human?*
- His final, desperate thought is to challenge Fate to a jousting contest rather than see "the seed of Banquo kings". *Does this image mean that we still admire him for his courage? Give reasons for your answer.*

(AO3) Context and ideas:

- The reality of kingship does not bring Macbeth the security that he anticipated. *Is this one aspect of the theme of appearance vs reality?*
- The England of 1606 was rife with plots (such as the recent Gunpowder Plot) intended to replace the Protestant James I with a Catholic monarch. Even a 'rightful' king like James might be worried, but part of Macbeth's insecurity is that others might follow his example of regicide. *Could Shakespeare be signalling that usurpers never prosper?*

Question:

How does Shakespeare present Macbeth's thoughts and feelings about being king in lines 50–76?

Macbeth	Bring them before us. *Exit Servant.*
	To be thus, is nothing, but to be safely thus.
	Our fears in Banquo stick deep,
	And in his royalty of nature reigns that
	Which would be feared. 'Tis much he dares, 55
	And, to that dauntless temper of his mind,
	He hath a wisdom that doth guide his valour
	To act in safety. There is none but he
	Whose being I do fear. And under him
	My genius is rebuked, as it is said 60
	Mark Antony's was by Caesar. He chid the sisters,
	When first they put the name of king upon me,
	And bade them speak to him. Then prophet-like,
	They hailed him father to a line of kings.
	Upon my head they placed a fruitless crown, 65
	And put a barren sceptre in my grip,
	Thence to be wrenched with an unlineal hand,
	No son of mine succeeding. If't be so,
	For Banquo's issue have I 'filed my mind:
	For them, the gracious Duncan have I murdered: 70
	Put rancours in the vessel of my peace
	Only for them: and mine eternal jewel
	Given to the common enemy of man,
	To make them kings: the seed of Banquo kings.
	Rather than so, come Fate, into the list, 75
	And champion me to th' utterance! — Who's there?

Enter Servant, and two Murderers.

Macbeth	*[To the servant.]*
	Now go to the door, and stay there till we call.

                                                 Exit Servant.

	Was it not yesterday we spoke together?
Murderers	It was, so please your highness.
Macbeth	Well then, 80
	Now have you considered of my speeches?
	Know that it was he, in the times past,
	Which held you so under fortune,
	Which you thought had been our innocent self.
	This I made good to you in our last conference, 85
	Passed in probation with you.
	How you were borne in hand, how crossed,
	The instruments, who wrought with them,
	And all things else that might
	To half a soul and to a notion crazed 90
	Say, "Thus did Banquo."
1st Murderer	You made it known to us.
Macbeth	I did so, and went further, which is now
	Our point of second meeting. Do you find
	Your patience so predominant in your nature, 95
	That you can let this go? Are you so gospelled,
	To pray for this good man and for his issue,

52 To be ... safely thus: To be king is nothing unless I keep the crown

53–5 Our fears in Banquo ... would be feared: I fear Banquo has a natural nobility that looks king-like

56 dauntless temper of his mind: brave nature

60–1 My genius ... Caesar: my guiding spirit is held back as Mark Antony's spirit was held back by Octavius Caesar's (in Roman times)

61 chid the sisters: told the Witches off

63 bade: told

65–6 fruitless crown ... my grip: they made me king but not the father of kings

67 Thence to be wrenched ... unlineal hand: the crown will be taken from me by someone else's children

69 'filed: defiled, polluted

71 Put rancours ... my peace: filled my calm mind with bitter thoughts

72 mine eternal jewel: my soul

73 the common enemy of man: the devil

75 Rather than so: rather than have that happen

75 list: tournament, contest

76 champion me to th' utterance!: I'll fight you to stop that prophesy coming true!

82 he: refers to Banquo

83 Which held you ... under fortune: Who kept you from the good luck you deserved

85 made ... conference: explained last time we talked

86 Passed in probation: proved

87–8 borne in hand ... with them: deceived and obstructed and how he did this

90–1 To half a soul ... Banquo": make Banquo's guilt clear even to a half-wit or a madman

94–6 Do you find ... gospelled: Are you going to let him get away with this? Are you so full of Christian charity

A

Macbeth and the murderers, A: 2001, B: summer 2010.

1 Both photos show similar body language, with Macbeth drawing the murderers to him. How does it affect the audience's attitude towards Macbeth that he no longer does his murders in person?

A: *l–r* Richard Attlee, Jasper Britton, Jan Knightley; B: *l–r* Michael Camp, Elliot Cowan, Craig Vye

B

	Whose heavy hand hath bowed you to the grave,	
	And beggared yours forever?	
1st Murderer	We are men, my liege.	100
Macbeth	Ay, in the catalogue ye go for men,	
	As hounds, and greyhounds, mongrels, spaniels, curs,	
	Shoughs, water-rugs, and demi-wolves are clept	
	All by the name of dogs. The valued file	
	Distinguishes the swift, the slow, the subtle,	105
	The house-keeper, the hunter, every one	
	According to the gift which bounteous nature	
	Hath in him closed, whereby he does receive	
	Particular addition, from the bill	
	That writes them all alike. And so of men.	110
	Now, if you have a station in the file,	
	Not i' th' worst rank of manhood, say 't,	
	And I will put that business in your bosoms	
	Whose execution takes your enemy off,	
	Grapples you to the heart and love of us,	115
	Who wear our health but sickly in his life,	
	Which in his death were perfect.	
2nd Murderer	I am one, my liege,	
	Whom the vile blows and buffets of the world	
	Have so incensed that I am reckless what	120
	I do to spite the world.	
1st Murderer	And I another,	
	So weary with disasters, tugged with fortune,	
	That I would set my life on any chance,	
	To mend it or be rid on't.	
Macbeth	Both of you	
	Know Banquo was your enemy.	125
Murderers	True, my lord.	
Macbeth	So is he mine, and in such bloody distance	
	That every minute of his being thrusts	
	Against my near'st of life. And though I could	
	With barefaced power sweep him from my sight,	130
	And bid my will avouch it, yet I must not,	
	For certain friends that are both his and mine,	
	Whose loves I may not drop, but wail his fall	
	Who I myself struck down. And thence it is	
	That I to your assistance do make love;	135
	Masking the business from the common eye	
	For sundry weighty reasons.	
2nd Murderer	We shall, my lord,	
	Perform what you command us.	
1st Murderer	Though our lives—	
Macbeth	Your spirits shine through you. Within this hour at most	140
	I will advise you where to plant yourselves,	141
	Acquaint you with the perfect spy o' th' time,	
	The moment on't, for't must be done tonight,	

98 **heavy hand … to the grave:** ill-treatment has almost killed you

99 **beggared yours:** left your family poor

101 **catalogue:** list of living things

103 **clept:** called
104 **valued file:** the list that sorts them by their qualities

106 **house-keeper:** watchdog
108 **Hath in him closed:** has given him
109-10 **Particular addition… all alike:** the qualities that make him stand out from the rest
111 **station in the file:** place in the list
112 **worst rank:** lowest level
113-5 **put that business … love of us:** outline a plan so you can kill your enemy and earn my favour
116-7 **Who wear … perfect:** For I will never be comfortable while he lives

119 **blows and buffets:** punches, awful setbacks
120 **incensed that I am reckless:** angry that I don't care

122 **tugged with fortune:** tossed about by fate
123 **set my life … chance:** take any gamble with my life
124 **To mend … on't:** to improve it or die

127 **bloody distance:** dangerous hostility (refers to space between fencers sword-fighting)
128-9 **thrusts … of life:** stabs my heart
130 **With barefaced … sight:** have him executed, because I am king
133 **loves I may not drop:** support I can't afford to lose
133-4 **but wail … struck down:** I'm arranging his death, but must seem upset by it
135 **to your … love:** ask you to help me
136 **Masking … common eye:** keeping it secret
137 **sundry weighty:** various important

140 **Your spirits … you:** You are clearly reliable

142 **perfect spy o' th' time:** the best time to do it

✔ Banquo suspects that Macbeth murdered Duncan.

✔ We see Macbeth as king.

✔ Macbeth fears Banquo for what he knows. He also fears Banquo's heirs will be kings, not his.

✔ Macbeth checks that Banquo and Fleance will be out after dark, and arranges for two men to murder them.

✔ What is different between planning the murder of Duncan, and planning the murder of Banquo?

Lady Macbeth and Macbeth, 2001.

Compare this photo of Macbeth and Lady Macbeth with those from the same production on page 32.

1 Are there any clues in the actors' body language to show that the balance of power is shifting in their relationship? Give reasons for your answer.

2 Can you find evidence in the text to suggest this change in the balance of power in the relationship between Macbeth and Lady Macbeth? Quote from the text to support your answer.

Eve Best and Jasper Britton

exam SKILLS

Target skill: analysing imagery

Question: How does Shakespeare reveal Macbeth's state of mind through his words in lines 15–28 and 39–59?

Macbeth's relationship with Lady Macbeth has changed. She requests "a few words" with a Macbeth who tries to 'keep alone' and her tone is subdued. She realises that their "desire is got without content" and instead of the fierce energy that persuaded Macbeth to murder is the vain hope (echoing Macbeth) that "What's done is done." Macbeth now does most of the talking, and keeps her ignorant of his plans.

Discuss how his speeches reveal his "torture of the mind" through their images:

- The creatures he mentions include the snake, scorpions, bats, the "shard-borne beetle" and crows. These are associated with "night's black agents."
  Does that include himself and the murderers?

- He is ready to destroy heaven and earth to escape from his nightmares. *Might a Jacobean audience think that killing a king unleashes universal disorder?*

- Life is but a "fitful fever" and Macbeth envies Duncan the sleep of death. *Where else in the play have sleep and death been linked?*

- He craves the cover of darkness and inverts the usual idea of goodness – "Things bad begun make good themselves by ill". *Is he now just an evil figure?*

1 Look back at the suggestions about analysing language on page 20. Do these suggestions help answer the question above?

2 How would you answer the question above?

And something from the palace, always thought
That I require a clearness. And with him, 145
To leave no rubs nor botches in the work,
Fleance, his son, that keeps him company,
Whose absence is no less material to me
Than is his father's, must embrace the fate
Of that dark hour. Resolve yourselves apart, 150
I'll come to you anon.

Murderers We are resolved, my lord.

Macbeth I'll call upon you straight. Abide within.—
It is concluded. Banquo, thy soul's flight,
If it find heaven, must find it out tonight. 155

Exit Macbeth and the Murderers.

ACT 3 SCENE 2

Enter Lady Macbeth and a Servant.

Lady Macbeth Is Banquo gone from court?

Servant Ay, madam, but returns again tonight.

Lady Macbeth Say to the king, I would attend his leisure
For a few words.

Servant Madam, I will.   *Exit Servant.* 5

Lady Macbeth Naught's had, all's spent,
Where our desire is got without content.
'Tis safer to be that which we destroy,
Than by destruction dwell in doubtful joy.

Enter Macbeth.

How now, my lord, why do you keep alone, 10
Of sorriest fancies your companions making,
Using those thoughts which should indeed have died
With them they think on? Things without all remedy
Should be without regard. What's done is done.

Macbeth We have scorched the snake, not killed it. 15
She'll close, and be herself, whilst our poor malice
Remains in danger of her former tooth.
But let the frame of things disjoint, both the worlds suffer,
Ere we will eat our meal in fear, and sleep
In the affliction of these terrible dreams 20
That shake us nightly. Better be with the dead,
Whom we, to gain our peace, have sent to peace,
Than on the torture of the mind to lie
In restless ecstasy. Duncan is in his grave.
After life's fitful fever he sleeps well, 25
Treason has done his worst: nor steel, nor poison,
Malice domestic, foreign levy, nothing
Can touch him further.

Lady Macbeth Come on,

144 **something:** some distance
144–5 **always thought ... clearness:** remember, I must not be suspected
146 **leave no rubs ... work:** don't make any mistakes
148 **material:** important
149–50 **embrace the fate ... hour:** die too
150 **Resolve yourselves apart:** Go and talk over your decision
151 **anon:** at once
153 **straight:** without delay
153 **Abide within:** Wait inside

3–4 **I would attend ... words:** I'd like to talk to him, as soon as it is convenient
6 **Naught's had, all's spent:** Nothing's gained, everything's wasted
7 **Where our desire ... content:** when getting what we want doesn't make us happy
8–9 **'Tis safer ... doubtful joy:** Better to be murdered than to be a murderer haunted by fear
11 **sorriest fancies:** the most painful thoughts
12–3 **Using those ... think on?:** thinking about the murder of Duncan
12–3 **Things without ...without regard:** if you can't change things, don't brood on them
15 **scorched:** slashed, wounded
16–7 **She'll close ... former tooth:** She'll heal and be a threat to us again
18 **let the frame ... the worlds:** disrupt the proper order of the universe and both heaven and earth
20 **affliction:** misery
22 **to gain ... sent to peace:** have murdered to get what we want
23–4 **on the torture ... ecstasy:** to lie in a frantic, sleepless, trance
25 **fitful fever:** restless, overheated, activity
27 **Malice domestic:** civil war
27 **foreign levy:** foreign invasion

59

Macbeth and Lady Macbeth in Act 2 Scene 2, watched by the Witches, summer 2010.

1 What change has the director made to Shakespeare's text for this scene?

2 Macbeth was speaking when the photo was taken. What line do you think he was saying? Give reasons for your answer.

l–r Elliot Cowan, Laura Rogers, Karen Anderson, Simone Kirby, Janet Fullerlove

Director's Note, 3.2

✔ Neither Lady Macbeth, nor Macbeth, is content.
✔ The audience know Macbeth has planned the murder of Banquo, but he chooses not to tell Lady Macbeth.
✔ How has Shakespeare shown their relationship changing?

Actor's view

Laura Rogers
Lady Macbeth, summer 2010

Interviewer: *Now, Macbeth makes a point of telling you there's something he is not going to tell you. For your Lady Macbeth, does this mark a change in the relationship?*

Laura Rogers: *Yes, definitely. Because, I think, they had been so close and everything, every decision they had made, they made together – or she had made and he would go along with it. She was the driving force, and she planted all the seeds in his head about what to do next, and suddenly, I think this is the first time, that she realizes that her power, her hold over him, isn't as strong anymore, because they had shared everything – he would not have a thought that she didn't know. Now, he was starting to* make plans by himself and keep her out of it. So, I think she starts to feel alienated, and like her control is slipping and that's when I think she starts to feel very vulnerable because without him she is nothing. So, if she feels that he is going away from her, in any sense, then she has nothing left and who knows what will happen next?! I don't suppose she felt very safe herself … are his thoughts … are they murderous thoughts? If so, who does he think he needs to kill? Maybe she is worried for her own life and, her own safety. And just the fact that, at that point, I suppose she feels that she is not as loved as she once was. And she finds herself in a very vulnerable position, which she doesn't know how to claw herself back from. Her manipulation isn't working any more.

	Gentle my lord, sleek o'er your rugged looks,	30
	Be bright and jovial among your guests tonight.	
Macbeth	So shall I love, and so I pray be you.	
	Let your remembrance apply to Banquo.	
	Present him eminence, both with eye and tongue:	
	Unsafe the while, that we must lave	35
	Our honours in these flattering streams;	
	And make our faces vizards to our hearts,	
	Disguising what they are.	
Lady Macbeth	You must leave this.	
Macbeth	O, full of scorpions is my mind, dear wife!	
	Thou know'st that Banquo and his Fleance lives.	40
Lady Macbeth	But in them nature's copy's not eterne.	
Macbeth	There's comfort yet, they are assailable,	
	Then be thou jocund. Ere the bat hath flown	
	His cloistered flight, ere to black Hecate's summons	
	The shard-borne beetle with his drowsy hums	45
	Hath rung night's yawning peal, there shall be done	
	A deed of dreadful note.	
Lady Macbeth	What's to be done?	
Macbeth	Be innocent of the knowledge, dearest chuck,	
	Till thou applaud the deed. — Come, seeling night,	
	Scarf up the tender eye of pitiful day;	50
	And with thy bloody and invisible hand	
	Cancel and tear to pieces that great bond	
	Which keeps me pale. Light thickens,	
	And the crow makes wing to th' rooky wood.	
	Good things of day begin to droop and drowse,	55
	Whiles night's black agents to their preys do rouse.	
	Thou marvell'st at my words: but hold thee still,	
	Things bad begun make strong themselves by ill.	
	So prithee go with me.	

Exit Macbeth and Lady Macbeth.

30 **sleek o'er:** smooth over
30 **rugged:** troubled, disturbed
33–4 **Let your remembrance ... eminence:** Remember to pay special attention to Banquo
35–6 **Unsafe the while ... streams:** We're not yet secure in our power and must use flattery to keep people on our side
37 **vizards:** masks
41 **in them nature's ... eterne:** they're human, they can't live forever
42 **assailable:** open to attack
43 **jocund:** cheerful
44 **cloistered:** restricted, habitual
44 **Hecate:** goddess of the moon and witchcraft
45–6 **shard-borne beetle ... peal:** dung beetle had brought the night (from an Ancient Egyptian myth)
49 **seeling:** blinding
50 **Scarf up:** blindfold
50 **pitiful:** sympathetic, compassionate
52–3 **Cancel and tear ... pale:** destroy Banquo and Fleance who threaten me (as in tearing up a legal document)
53 **Light thickens:** It's getting darker
56 **night's black agents... rouse:** evil things start hunting
57 **hold thee still:** wait and see
58 **Things bad begun ... ill:** evil deeds have to be followed by more evil deeds

exam SKILLS

Target skill: analysing character presentation

Question: How does Shakespeare present the changing relationship between Macbeth and Lady Macbeth in lines 15–55?

Before answering the question, read the extract carefully; it may help to make notes. Study the points below. Do you agree or disagree with them, or are they irrelevant?

- Both realise their "desire is got without content".
- Macbeth calls Lady Macbeth his "dear wife" but they are no longer partners; now he does the talking.
- Lady Macbeth lacks her earlier passionate power.
- The plan to kill Banquo is Macbeth's alone.
- We respond differently because have witnessed Macbeth's devious manipulation of the murderers.
- Macbeth's royal world is one of nightmare and fear – "full of scorpions is my mind".
- Lady Macbeth's language is unimaginative.
- The contest between good and evil is a major theme: Macbeth is now aligned with darkness and evil.

The murderers attack – Banquo (centre, kicking) fights them off while Fleance (crouching) escapes, 2013.

Critic A: "There is no tension in this scene. We already know that Banquo will die, and that Fleance will escape."

Critic B: "Shakespeare carefully builds the tension in this scene. An unknown third man joins the two murderers. Their conversation is strained as they wait for Banquo and Fleance. Then Banquo shouts from offstage, and the action explodes in the last ten lines."

Which of these critics do you agree with? Give reasons for your answer.

Geoff Aymer, Jonathan Chambers, Colin Ryan, Billy Boyd, Harry Hepple

Director's Note, 3.3

✔ The Murderers lie in wait for Banquo and Fleance.
✔ They attack in the dark, but Fleance escapes.
✔ What does Shakespeare do to show Macbeth's growing distrust of everybody?

Enter three Murderers.

1st Murderer	But who did bid thee join with us?
3rd Murderer	Macbeth.
2nd Murderer	He needs not our mistrust, since he delivers Our offices, and what we have to do, To the direction just.
1st Murderer	Then stand with us.

5 The west yet glimmers with some streaks of day.
Now spurs the lated traveller apace
To gain the timely inn, and near approaches
The subject of our watch.

3rd Murderer	Hark, I hear horses.
Banquo	*Within* Give us a light there, ho.

10

2nd Murderer	Then 'tis he. The rest That are within the note of expectation Already are i' th' court.
1st Murderer	His horses go about.
3rd Murderer	Almost a mile: but he does usually,

15 So all men do, from hence to th' palace gate
Make it their walk.

Enter Fleance with a torch, and Banquo.

2nd Murderer	A light, a light!
3rd Murderer	'Tis he.
1st Murderer	Stand to 't.

20

Banquo	It will be rain tonight.
1st Murderer	Let it come down.

[The Murderers attack. The torch goes out.]

Banquo	O, treachery! Fly good Fleance, fly, fly, fly! Thou mayst revenge. — O slave!

25

[Banquo is killed. Fleance escapes.]

3rd Murderer	Who did strike out the light?
1st Murderer	Was't not the way?
3rd Murderer	There's but one down. The son is fled.
2nd Murderer	We have lost best half of our affair.
3rd Murderer	Well, let's away, and say how much is done.

Exit the three Murderers.

2–3 **He needs not our mistrust ... offices:** We can trust him, he knows our orders

4 **To the direction just:** exactly

5 **yet:** still, even now

6–7 **spurs the lated ... inn:** travellers still on the road hurry to reach the inn before dark

8 **The subject of our watch:** those we're waiting for (Banquo and Fleance)

12 **within expectation:** invited to the banquet

14 **go about:** are being led to the stables

20 **Stand to 't:** Get ready

22 **Let it come down:** referring to the rain and the attack

25 **Thou mayst ... slave:** Live to revenge my murder (to Fleance). You villain (to the Murderer)

26 **Was't not the way?:** Wasn't that the plan?

28 **lost best ... affair:** let the most important victim escape

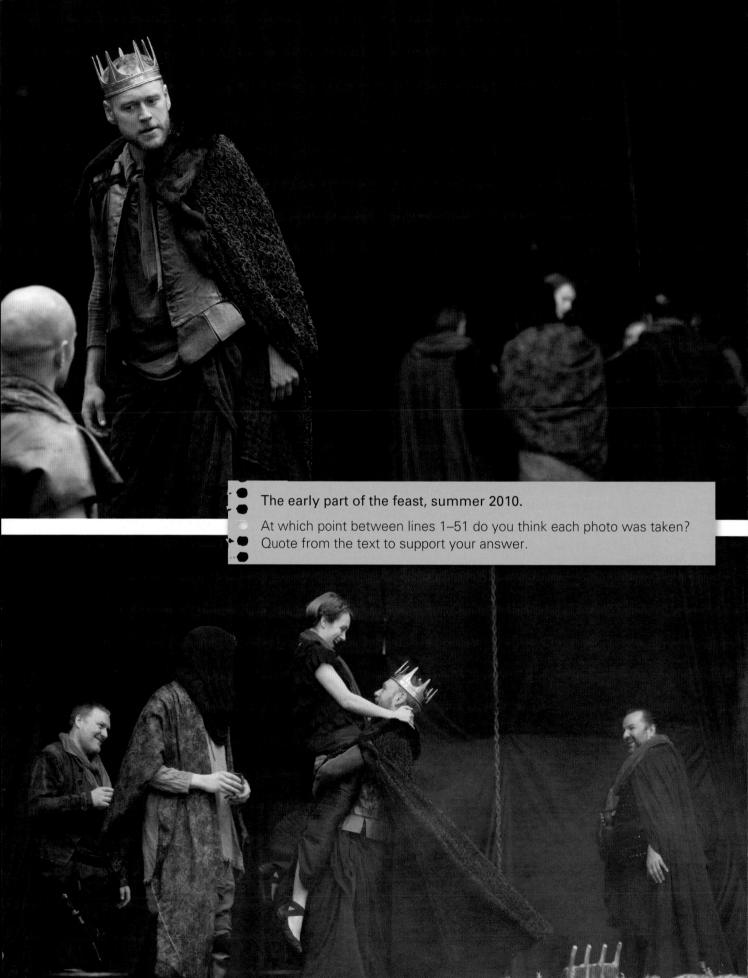

The early part of the feast, summer 2010.

At which point between lines 1–51 do you think each photo was taken? Quote from the text to support your answer.

A banquet is set out.
Enter Macbeth, Lady Macbeth, Ross, Lennox, other Lords,
and attendants.

Macbeth	You know your own degrees, sit down. At first and last the hearty welcome.
Lords	Thanks to your majesty.
Macbeth	Ourself will mingle with society, And play the humble host. 5 Our hostess keeps her state, but in best time We will require her welcome.
Lady Macbeth	Pronounce it for me, sir, to all our friends, For my heart speaks, they are welcome.

Enter first Murderer, inconspicuously.

Macbeth	See, they encounter thee with their hearts' thanks. 10 Both sides are even. Here I'll sit i' th' midst. Be large in mirth, anon we'll drink a measure The table round. *[To the Murderer.]* There's blood upon thy face.
1st Murderer	'Tis Banquo's then.
Macbeth	'Tis better thee without than he within. 15 Is he despatched?
1st Murderer	My lord, his throat is cut, that I did for him.
Macbeth	Thou art the best o' th' cut-throats, Yet he's good that did the like for Fleance. If thou didst it, thou art the nonpareil. 20
1st Murderer	Most royal sir, Fleance is 'scaped.
Macbeth	Then comes my fit again. I had else been perfect; Whole as the marble, founded as the rock; As broad and general as the casing air. But now I am cabined, cribbed, confined, bound in 25 To saucy doubts and fears. — But Banquo's safe?
1st Murderer	Ay, my good lord. Safe in a ditch he bides, With twenty trenchèd gashes on his head, The least a death to nature.
Macbeth	Thanks for that. — There the grown serpent lies, the worm that's fled 30 Hath nature that in time will venom breed, No teeth for th' present. — Get thee gone, tomorrow We'll hear ourselves again. *Exit Murderer.*
Lady Macbeth	My royal lord, You do not give the cheer. The feast is sold That is not often vouched while 'tis a-making. 35 'Tis given with welcome. To feed were best at home: From thence, the sauce to meat is ceremony,

1 **degrees:** social importance (this affected where you could sit)
2 **At first and last the:** to everyone a

4 **society:** everyone here

6–7 **keeps … welcome:** will sit in her place at the table until the right time to welcome you
8 **Pronounce it for me:** Say it for me

10 **encounter thee:** respond
11 **Both sides are even:** There are the same number of people on each side of the table
12 **Be large in mirth:** enjoy yourselves
12 **measure … round:** all drink a toast
15 **'Tis better … within:** better on you than still inside him
16 **despatched:** killed

20 **the nonpareil:** unequalled

21 **is 'scaped:** has escaped

22 **my fit:** my fears and doubts
24 **perfect:** completely satisfied
23–4 **Whole as … air:** solid as marble, stable as rock and free as air
25–6 **cabined, cribbed … saucy:** imprisoned by my uncontrollable
26 **safe:** definitely dead
27 **bides:** will stay
28 **trenchèd:** cut deep (like a trench)
29 **The least … nature:** the smallest of which would have killed him
30 **grown serpent:** Banquo
30 **worm:** young snake (referring to Fleance)
31–2 **Hath nature … present:** will be trouble later, but is harmless for now
33 **hear ourselves:** talk
34 **give the cheer:** act like a good host
34–8 **The feast … without it:**

Macbeth's nobles at the feast, upper, spring 2010 (Macbeth is on the right-hand edge of the photo) and, lower, summer 2010.

Was each photo taken before or after Macbeth sees the ghost (line 52)? Quote from the text to support your answer.

Meeting were bare without it.

Enter the Ghost of Banquo. He sits in Macbeth's place and is invisible to Lady Macbeth and the Lords.

Macbeth   Sweet remembrancer!
Now, good digestion wait on appetite,   40
And health on both!

Lennox   May't please your highness sit.

Macbeth   Here had we now our country's honour, roofed,
Were the graced person of our Banquo present.
Who may I rather challenge for unkindness
Than pity for mischance.

Ross   His absence, sir,   45
Lays blame upon his promise. Please't your highness
To grace us with your royal company?

Macbeth   The table's full.

Lennox   Here is a place reserved, sir.

Macbeth   Where?   50

Lennox   Here, my good lord.

[Macbeth sees the Ghost of Banquo.]

What is't that moves your highness?

Macbeth   Which of you have done this?

Lennox   What, my good lord?

Macbeth   Thou canst not say I did it. Never shake
Thy gory locks at me.   55

Ross   Gentlemen, rise, his highness is not well.

Lady Macbeth   Sit worthy friends. My lord is often thus,
And hath been from his youth. Pray you keep seat,
The fit is momentary, upon a thought
He will again be well. If much you note him   60
You shall offend him, and extend his passion.
Feed, and regard him not. — Are you a man?

Macbeth   Ay, and a bold one, that dare look on that
Which might appal the devil.

Lady Macbeth   O proper stuff!   65
This is the very painting of your fear.
This is the air-drawn dagger which you said
Led you to Duncan. O, these flaws, and starts,
Impostors to true fear, would well become
A woman's story at a winter's fire,   70
Authorized by her grandam. Shame itself,
Why do you make such faces? When all's done,
You look but on a stool.

Notes:

people will feel they are eating out for payment, not with friends. Unless you make them feel at home, they might as well have stayed at home

39 **Sweet remembrancer:** Thank you for reminding me, sweetheart

42 **country's honour:** most important lords in Scotland
42 **roofed:** under the same roof
43 **graced:** worthy, gifted
44-5 **Who may I ... mischance:** who I hope is just rudely late, then I can tell him off, not come to harm
45-6 **His ... promise:** He shouldn't have promised to come if he thought he might not be able to get here

52 **moves:** upsets

54 **Thou canst not say I did it:** you can't say I murdered you
55 **gory locks:** hair caked in blood

59 **upon a thought:** in a moment
60 **much ... him:** you stare at him
61 **extend his passion:** make his fit last longer

65 **proper stuff:** nonsense
66 **the very painting ... fear:** something your fear has made you imagine
67 **flaws:** emotional outbursts
67 **starts:** jerks, twitches
69 **Impostors to true fear:** are nothing compared to real fear
70-1 **A woman's story ... grandam:** an old wives' tale

Lady Macbeth, Macbeth and Banquo's Ghost, 2001.

1 How have the director and designer chosen to show that this is a banquet?

2 What issues does a director need to think about when staging the ghost?

3 Look back at the photos on page 66 as well. You can see three different ways of staging the ghost. What issues are raised by this range of interpretations?

Eve Best, Patrick Brennan (blindfolded) and Jasper Britton

Actor's view

James Garnon
Macbeth, spring 2010

I think the only intelligent response is that Macbeth imagines that the Ghost is real; it's real for Macbeth. And I suppose beyond that the only other thing that's interesting about it is that Macbeth imagines that it's real for everyone else, when it obviously isn't. No one else appears to see it, but he appears to see in them that they have, given his reaction to them at the end of the scene. Clearly ghosts are real to Macbeth – that's all we need to know.

In this particular case Banquo's ghost seems to drive him on to a further acceptance of his own nature, a further acceptance of how much he has changed, how much he has moved on; it has driven him to a point where he can contemplate further murders, bizarrely. You think you'd be visited by the ghost and he would then be horrified and cease, but in fact he's horrified, and goes on. Immediately he starts talking about what he's going to do to Macduff.

Actor's view

Julius D'Silva
Ross, summer 2010

We have a large platter, an enormous platter of roasted meats, and fruit and legs of lamb and hams, and you see the platter come onstage with nothing underneath it, rather like the old magic tricks. And then you see a hand, a bloody hand come out of it and grab Macbeth's hand as he leans over the platter of meat, which gets a gasp from the audience. And then gradually you see him pull the ghost of Banquo, as if by magic, out of this platter of bloody meat. And you see Banquo come out from the middle of it, and it's completely unexpected, and it gets a great reaction from the audience.

The hard bit for the actor is of course, not noticing him! Elliot [Cowan, Macbeth] is the only actor who can see Banquo. So we have to follow each others' eye line and we have to be concerned with Macbeth in that moment to try not to stare at this 6 foot 2 man covered in tomato ketchup, who's wandering round the stage.

But it's a great moment and I think one of the most dramatic moments in the whole production really.

Macbeth	Prithee see there!

Macbeth
Prithee see there!
Behold! Look! Lo! How say you?
Why what care I? If thou canst nod, speak too. 75
If charnel houses and our graves must send
Those that we bury, back; our monuments
Shall be the maws of kites. *[Exit Ghost of Banquo.]*

Lady Macbeth What, quite unmanned in folly?

Macbeth If I stand here, I saw him.

Lady Macbeth Fie, for shame! 80

Macbeth Blood hath been shed ere now, i' th' olden time,
Ere human statute purged the gentle weal.
Ay, and since too, murders have been performed
Too terrible for the ear. The time has been,
That when the brains were out, the man would die, 85
And there an end. But now they rise again,
With twenty mortal murders on their crowns,
And push us from our stools. This is more strange
Than such a murder is.

Lady Macbeth My worthy lord,
Your noble friends do lack you.

Macbeth I do forget. 90
Do not muse at me my most worthy friends,
I have a strange infirmity, which is nothing
To those that know me. Come, love and health to all,
Then I'll sit down. — Give me some wine, fill full. —

Enter Ghost of Banquo.

I drink to th' general joy o' th' whole table, 95
And to our dear friend Banquo, whom we miss.
Would he were here! To all, and him, we thirst,
And all to all.

Lords Our duties, and the pledge.

Macbeth *[He sees the Ghost of Banquo.]*
Avaunt, and quit my sight! Let the earth hide thee!
Thy bones are marrowless, thy blood is cold. 100
Thou hast no speculation in those eyes
Which thou dost glare with.

Lady Macbeth Think of this, good peers,
But as a thing of custom. 'Tis no other,
Only it spoils the pleasure of the time.

Macbeth What man dare, I dare. 105
Approach thou like the rugged Russian bear,
The armed rhinoceros, or th' Hyrcan tiger,
Take any shape but that, and my firm nerves
Shall never tremble. Or be alive again,
And dare me to the desert with thy sword. 110
If trembling I inhabit then, protest me
The baby of a girl. Hence, horrible shadow!
Unreal mock'ry hence! *[Exit Ghost of Banquo.]*

73 Prithee: for heaven's sake
76 charnel houses: places where the bones of the dead were stored
77-8 monuments ... kites: tombs will be the stomachs of the birds who feed off the dead
79 What ... folly?: Has your madness made you lose your manly courage?
81 ere: before
82 Ere human statute ... weal: before people made laws to control behaviour
87 mortal murders ... crowns: fatal head wounds
90 do lack you: miss your company
91 muse: be surprised, wonder
92 infirmity: illness
97 thirst: drink
98 And all to all: and good health to everyone
98 Our duties, and the pledge: We confirm our loyalty to you and toast you in return
99 Avaunt: Go!
101 speculation: sight
103 But as a thing of custom: as a regular event
106 rugged: hairy, shaggy
107 Hyrcan: from Hyrcania (south of the Caspian Sea), a wild place famous for tigers
108 but that: except Banquo's ghost
110 to the desert: to a fight to the death in a lonely place
111-2 If trembling ... girl: If I stay trembling indoors then, call me a helpless doll

Director's Note, 3.4

✔ As Macbeth entertains his nobles at a banquet, the Murderer reports that Banquo is dead, but Fleance escaped.
✔ He rejoins the banquet, then sees Banquo's Ghost. Nobody else can see it, or understand Macbeth's behaviour.
✔ Lady Macbeth tries to cover up, saying it is an old illness, but, just as he recovers, Macbeth sees the Ghost again.
✔ Again the nobles are worried, and this time Lady Macbeth tells them to leave.
✔ When they are alone, Macbeth decides to visit the Witches for more prophesies.
✔ What effect will these events have on the nobles' view of Macbeth as King?

exam PREPARATION

Text focus: Act 3 Scene 4 lines 95–127

(AO1) Response to characters and events:
- Macbeth sees the ghost while his wife struggles to understand what amazes him. Macbeth cannot understand why she is not terrified too. *Why does Shakespeare have only Macbeth seeing the ghost?*
- Why might Shakespeare have chosen to have Banquo's ghost terrify Macbeth rather than Duncan's ghost?
- The calmness of Lady Macbeth contrasts with Macbeth's haunted shrieks. *How does Shakespeare show her trying to keep control? Does it work?*

(AO2) Language, structure and form:
- Macbeth's exclaims with horror at the sight of "blood boltered Banquo". *When was he fearful of blood before?*
- Shakespeare shows Macbeth, a brave warrior, as scared in this scene. *How does he do this?*

- The change in tone and pace when the ghost leaves is extraordinary – "Why, so, being gone, I am a man again. – Pray you, sit still." *What impact might this change in tone have on the audience?*

(AO3) Context and ideas:
- The supernatural plays a major part in the play, suggesting that there is a world beyond the world of men. *What might a modern audience think of Banquo's ghost?*

Question:
How does Shakespeare present Macbeth's thoughts and feelings during lines 95–127?

	Why, so, being gone, I am a man again. — Pray you, sit still.
Lady Macbeth	You have displaced the mirth, 115 Broke the good meeting, with most admired disorder.
Macbeth	Can such things be, And overcome us like a summer's cloud, Without our special wonder? You make me strange Even to the disposition that I owe, 120 When now I think you can behold such sights, And keep the natural ruby of your cheeks, When mine is blanched with fear.
Ross	What sights, my lord?
Lady Macbeth	I pray you speak not. He grows worse and worse. Question enrages him. At once, good-night. 125 Stand not upon the order of your going, But go at once.
Lennox	Good night, and better health Attend his majesty.
Lady Macbeth	A kind good night to all.

Exit all but Macbeth and Lady Macbeth.

Macbeth	It will have blood they say. Blood will have blood. 130 Stones have been known to move, and trees to speak. Augurs, and understood relations, have By magot-pies and choughs and rooks brought forth The secret'st man of blood. — What is the night?
Lady Macbeth	Almost at odds with morning, which is which. 135
Macbeth	How say'st thou that Macduff denies his person At our great bidding?
Lady Macbeth	Did you send to him, sir?
Macbeth	I hear it by the way, but I will send. There's not a one of them but in his house 140 I keep a servant fee'd. I will tomorrow (And betimes I will) to the weird sisters. More shall they speak. For now I am bent to know By the worst means, the worst. For mine own good, All causes shall give way. I am in blood 145 Stepped in so far, that should I wade no more, Returning were as tedious as go o'er. Strange things I have in head, that will to hand, Which must be acted, ere they may be scanned.
Lady Macbeth	You lack the season of all natures, sleep. 150
Macbeth	Come, we'll to sleep. My strange and self-abuse Is the initiate fear that wants hard use. We are yet but young in deed. *They exit.*

Glossary

112 **shadow:** ghost

115 **displaced the mirth:** spoiled everyone's evening

116 **most admired disorder:** disturbing behaviour no one could ignore

119 **Without our special wonder?:** without me noticing and reacting to it

119-23 **You make me ... blanched with fear:** I thought I was brave but this vision has made me white with fear yet you look at it unmoved

126 **Stand ... going:** don't go in order of importance, just go quickly

130 **It will have blood... Blood will have blood:** murder will lead to more murder

132 **Augers ... relations:** prophesies and knowing how events are connected

133 **magot-pies ... rooks:** magpies, crows and rooks (birds foretelling bad luck)

133-4 **brought forth ... man of blood:** revealed the most cunning hidden murderers

135 **Almost at odds ... which is which:** somewhere between night and day

136 **How say'st thou:** What do you think of the fact that

136-7 **denies his person ... bidding?:** chose not to come to court, despite my command to do so?

139 **by the way:** from my spies

140 **them:** the nobles

141 **fee'd:** paid (to spy)

142 **betimes:** very early

143 **bent:** determined

144 **by the worst means:** by witchcraft

144 **For mine own good:** to get what I want

146 **should:** even if

148 **in head:** planned

148 **to hand:** be done

149 **acted, ere ... scanned:** carried out before I can think about them too hard

150 **season of all natures:** the thing we need to keep us fresh

151 **self-abuse:** self-deception

152 **initiate:** beginner's

152 **wants hard use:** needs practice

153 **young in deed:** new to murder

ACT 3 SCENE 5

Thunder. Enter three Witches, meeting Hecate.

First Witch   Why, how now Hecate, you look angerly.

Hecate   Have I not reason, beldams, as you are?
Saucy and overbold, how did you dare
To trade and traffic with Macbeth,
In riddles and affairs of death?   5
And I, the mistress of your charms,
The close contriver of all harms,
Was never called to bear my part,
Or show the glory of our art?
And which is worse, all you have done   10
Hath been but for a wayward son,
Spiteful and wrathful who, as others do,
Loves for his own ends, not for you.
But make amends now. Get you gone,
And at the pit of Acheron   15
Meet me i' th' morning. Thither he
Will come to know his destiny.
Your vessels and your spells provide,
Your charms and everything beside.
I am for th' air. This night I'll spend   20
Unto a dismal and a fatal end.
Great business must be wrought ere noon.
Upon the corner of the moon
There hangs a vap'rous drop, profound,
I'll catch it ere it come to ground;   25
And that distilled by magic sleights,
Shall raise such artificial sprites,
As by the strength of their illusion,
Shall draw him on to his confusion.
He shall spurn fate, scorn death, and bear   30
His hopes 'bove wisdom, grace and fear.
And you all know, security
Is mortals' chiefest enemy.

Music and a song.

Hark, I am called. My little spirit, see,
Sits in a foggy cloud and stays for me.   *[Exit Hecate.]* 35

A song within, "Come away, come away" etc.

First Witch   Come, let's make haste; she'll soon be back again.

Exit the three Witches.

ACT 3 SCENE 6

Enter Lennox and another Lord.

Lennox   My former speeches have but hit your thoughts
Which can interpret farther. Only I say
Things have been strangely borne. The gracious Duncan

SHAKESPEARE'S WORLD
◇◇◇◇◇◇◇◇◇◇◇◇

Authorship
Shakespeare probably didn't write this scene. When Shakespeare's company, the King's Men, put an old play on again, they often added some new scenes, so more people would come to watch it again. After Shakespeare died, another playwright, Thomas Middleton, revised *Macbeth* for the King's Men. Middleton probably added two songs and a dance to *Macbeth*. Hecate's song, 'Come, away…' is also in Middleton's play *The Witch* (1616).

1 **Hecate:** goddess of the moon and witchcraft
2 **beldams:** witches
3 **trade and traffic:** have dealings with
6 **charms:** spells, magic
7 **close contriver:** secret arranger
11 **wayward son:** unreliable ally (Macbeth)
15 **pit of Acheron:** part of Hell
16 **Thither:** There
18 **vessels:** containers (their cauldron)
21 **Unto a dismal … end:** planning something evil and deadly
22 **wrought:** done
24 **vap'rous drop:** foggy drop said to be from the moon to be used in spells
25 **profound:** so full it is about to fall to Earth
26 **distilled by magic sleights:** strengthened by magic skills
27 **artificial sprites:** unreal spirits
28 **illusion:** ability to trick
29 **confusion:** ruin, overthrow
30 **spurn:** reject
30–1 **bear His hopes 'bove:** hopes that make him act against
32 **security:** feeling confident, safe
32 **mortals:** humans
35 **stays:** waits

1–2 **My former speeches … farther:** we are in agreement
3 **been strangely borne:** turned out oddly

Was pitied of Macbeth, marry, he was dead.
And the right valiant Banquo walked too late, 5
Whom, you may say (if't please you) Fleance killed,
For Fleance fled. Men must not walk too late.
Who cannot want the thought, how monstrous
It was for Malcolm and for Donalbain
To kill their gracious father? Damnèd fact, 10
How it did grieve Macbeth! Did he not straight
In pious rage, the two delinquents tear,
That were the slaves of drink and thralls of sleep?
Was not that nobly done? Ay, and wisely too.
For 'twould have angered any heart alive 15
To hear the men deny't. So that I say
He has borne all things well. And I do think
That had he Duncan's sons under his key,
(As, an't please heaven, he shall not) they should find
What 'twere to kill a father. So should Fleance. 20
But peace, for from broad words, and 'cause he failed
His presence at the tyrant's feast, I hear
Macduff lives in disgrace. Sir, can you tell
Where he bestows himself?

Lord The son of Duncan, 25
From whom this tyrant holds the due of birth,
Lives in the English court, and is received
Of the most pious Edward with such grace,
That the malevolence of fortune nothing
Takes from his high respect. Thither Macduff 30
Is gone, to pray the holy king upon his aid
To wake Northumberland and warlike Siward.
That, by the help of these (with Him above
To ratify the work) we may again
Give to our tables meat, sleep to our nights, 35
Free from our feasts and banquets bloody knives,
Do faithful homage and receive free honours,
All which we pine for now. And this report
Hath so exasperate the king that he
Prepares for some attempt of war. 40

Lennox Sent he to Macduff?

Lord He did. And with an absolute "Sir, not I."
The cloudy messenger turns me his back,
And hums, as who should say, "You'll rue the time
That clogs me with this answer." 45

Lennox And that well might
Advise him to a caution, t'hold what distance
His wisdom can provide. Some holy angel
Fly to the court of England and unfold
His message ere he come, that a swift blessing 50
May soon return to this our suffering country
Under a hand accursed.

Lord I'll send my prayers with him.

Exit Lennox and the Lord.

---

8 **want the thought:** help thinking

10 **fact:** action (the murder)
11 **straight:** at once
12 **pious:** loyal, devoted
12 **two delinquents:** Duncan's servants
13 **thralls:** prisoners

17 **borne:** done
18 **under his key:** locked up
19 **an't:** if it
21 **from broad words:** because he spoke what he thought, unguardedly
21-2 **failed His presence … feast:** he didn't go to Macbeth's banquet
24 **bestows himself?:** is staying
26 **holds:** withholds, keeps away from
26 **due of birth:** the crown he should have inherited
28 **pious Edward:** King Edward the Confessor, known for his devotion to religion
28 **grace:** kindness, favour
29 **malevolence of fortune:** loss of his kingdom
29-30 **nothing Takes from … respect:** hasn't stopped him being treated with great respect
31 **upon his aid:** to help Malcolm
32 **wake:** call to war
33 **Him above:** God
34 **ratify:** approve
36 **Free from:** remove from
37 **Do faithful … free honours:** show loyalty to a king who will reward us for it
38 **pine:** long for
39 **exasperate:** angered
39 **the king:** Macbeth
43 **cloudy:** unhappy
43 **turns … back:** turns away
44-5 **hums, as … answer":** as if he wanted to say, "you'll regret that answer"
47 **Advise him to a caution:** warn Macduff to take care
47-8 **t'hold what distance … provide:** to keep as far from Macbeth as possible
52 **Under a hand accursed:** ruled by a hateful king (Macbeth)

ACT 4 SCENE 1

Thunder. Enter the three Witches.

First Witch	Thrice the brinded cat hath mewed.
Second Witch	Thrice, and once the hedge-pig whined.
Third Witch	Harpier cries — 'Tis time, 'tis time.
First Witch	Round about the cauldron go:
	In the poisoned entrails throw.
	Toad, that under cold stone
	Days and nights has thirty-one,
	Sweltered venom sleeping got,
	Boil thou first i' th' charmèd pot!
All	Double, double, toil and trouble;
	Fire burn, and cauldron bubble.
Second Witch	Fillet of a fenny snake,
	In the cauldron boil and bake.
	Eye of newt, and toe of frog,
	Wool of bat, and tongue of dog,
	Adder's fork, and blind-worm's sting,
	Lizard's leg, and howlet's wing.
	For a charm of powerful trouble,
	Like a hell-broth, boil and bubble.
All	Double, double, toil and trouble,
	Fire burn, and cauldron bubble.
Third Witch	Scale of dragon, tooth of wolf,
	Witch's mummy, maw and gulf

5

10

15

20

1 **Thrice:** Three times
1 **brinded:** striped
2 **hedge-pig:** hedgehog
3 **Harpier:** the third witch's 'familiar' – her link to the world of magic, disguised as an animal
5 **entrails:** guts
8 **Sweltered venom:** poison, sweated by the toad
9 **sleeping got:** taken while it slept
12 **Fillet:** a thick slice of
12 **fenny:** from the Fens, which are marshy and muddy
15 **Wool:** hair
16 **fork:** tongue
16 **blind-worm:** slow-worm
17 **howlet:** young owl
23 **mummy:** a powder made from Egyptian mummies
23 **maw and gulf:** throat and stomach

The Witches dance around the cauldron, spring 2010.

What effect might Shakespeare have intended by the language used by the Witches?

l–r Rachel Winters, Karen Bryson, Shane Zaza

Of the ravined salt-sea shark,
Root of hemlock, digged i' th' dark,   25
Liver of blaspheming Jew,
Gall of goat, and slips of yew
Slivered in the moon's eclipse,
Nose of Turk, and Tartar's lips,
Finger of birth-strangled babe   30
Ditch-delivered by a drab,
Make the gruel thick and slab.
Add thereto a tiger's chaudron,
For th' ingredients of our cauldron.

All   Double, double, toil and trouble,   35
Fire burn, and cauldron bubble.

Second Witch   Cool it with a baboon's blood,
Then the charm is firm and good.

Enter Hecate, and three other Witches.

Hecate   O well done! I commend your pains,
And every one shall share i' th' gains.   40
And now about the cauldron sing,
Like elves and fairies in a ring,
Enchanting all that you put in.

*Music, they sing a song, putting in more ingredients as they
dance round the cauldron.*

Second Witch   By the pricking of my thumbs,
Something wicked this way comes.   45

Exit Hecate and the other three witches.

Open, locks, whoever knocks!

Enter Macbeth.

Macbeth   How now, you secret, black and midnight hags?
What is't you do?

All   A deed without a name.

Macbeth   I conjure you, by that which you profess,
Howe'er you come to know it, answer me.   50
Though you untie the winds and let them fight
Against the churches, though the yeasty waves
Confound and swallow navigation up,
Though bladed corn be lodged, and trees blown down,
Though castles topple on their warders' heads   55
Though palaces and pyramids do slope
Their heads to their foundations, though the treasure
Of nature's germens tumble all together,
Even till destruction sicken. Answer me
To what I ask you.   60

First Witch   Speak.

Second Witch   Demand.

Third Witch   We'll answer.

24 **ravined:** full to bursting
25 **hemlock:** a poisonous plant
26 **blaspheming:** denying Christian beliefs
27 **Gall:** bitter liquid from the liver
27 **slips:** small twigs
28 **Slivered:** cut
29–30 **Turk … Tartar … birth-strangled babe:** none of these were baptised Christian, so the Witches could use them
31 **Ditch-delivered:** born in a ditch
31 **drab:** prostitute
32 **slab:** sticky
33 **chaudron:** guts

39 **commend your pains:** praise you for the trouble you have taken

49 **conjure:** demand

51 **Though:** Even if
51–2 **untie … churches:** send storms to knock down churches
52 **yeasty:** frothy
53 **Confound:** smash up
53 **navigation:** ships at sea
54 **bladed corn be lodged:** ripening corn is blown flat (and so ruined)
55 **warders:** people in charge
56 **slope:** bend
57–8 **the treasure … all together:** the elements that bring life itself are thrown into chaos
59 **sicken:** feels sick with overeating

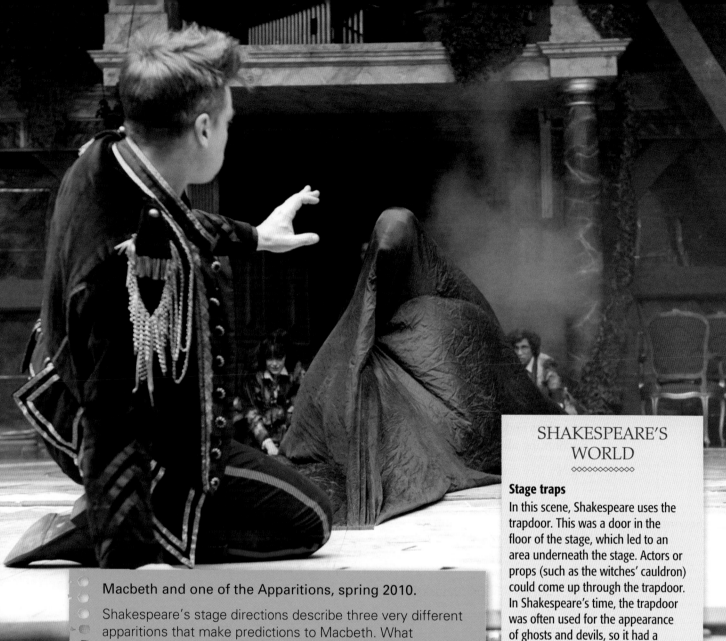

Macbeth and one of the Apparitions, spring 2010.

Shakespeare's stage directions describe three very different apparitions that make predictions to Macbeth. What challenges might these descriptions present to someone wanting to stage *Macbeth* at the Globe Theatre?

James Garnon

SHAKESPEARE'S WORLD

Stage traps

In this scene, Shakespeare uses the trapdoor. This was a door in the floor of the stage, which led to an area underneath the stage. Actors or props (such as the witches' cauldron) could come up through the trapdoor. In Shakespeare's time, the trapdoor was often used for the appearance of ghosts and devils, so it had a strong association with Hell or the Underworld. By using the trapdoor here, Shakespeare was hinting that the Witches were supernatural beings.

exam SKILLS

Target skill: commenting on Shakespeare's use of spectacle

Question: How might a modern audience react to apparitions that appear during lines 75–128?

Shakespeare opens the scene with the witches' disgusting but hypnotic spells of evil.

How far do you agree with these statements:

1 Macbeth is brave in demanding answers of an "unknown power".

2 The first apparition warns Macbeth, while the next two seem to reassure him. He believes all three.

3 It is the vision of Banquo's issue inheriting the crown that enrages Macbeth and makes him determined to slaughter the families of his opponents.

4 The Witches may influence Macbeth but they do not control him.

5 The apparitions would have appealed to a Jacobean audience's love of spectacle.

6 Using the apparitions was part of Shakespeare's exploration of the relationship between appearance and reality.

First Witch	Say, if th' hadst rather hear it from our mouths,
	Or from our masters? 65
Macbeth	Call 'em. Let me see 'em.
First Witch	Pour in sow's blood that hath eaten
	Her nine farrow, grease that's sweaten
	From the murderer's gibbet, throw
	Into the flame. 70
All	Come high or low:
	Thyself and office deftly show! *Thunder.*

An Apparition appears, it is a head wearing armour.

Macbeth	Tell me, thou unknown power.
First Witch	He knows thy thought.
	Hear his speech, but say thou naught.
1st Apparition	Macbeth, Macbeth, Macbeth! Beware Macduff! 75
	Beware the Thane of Fife! Dismiss me. Enough.

1st Apparition descends.

Macbeth	Whate'er thou art, for thy good caution, thanks.
	Thou hast harped my fear aright. But one word more.
First Witch	He will not be commanded. Here's another,
	More potent than the first. *Thunder.* 80

2nd Apparition appears, it is a bloody child.

2nd Apparition	Macbeth, Macbeth, Macbeth!
Macbeth	Had I three ears, I'd hear thee.
2nd Apparition	Be bloody, bold, and resolute. Laugh to scorn
	The power of man, for none of woman born
	Shall harm Macbeth. 85

2nd Apparition descends.

Macbeth	Then live Macduff: what need I fear of thee?
	But yet I'll make assurance double sure,
	And take a bond of fate. Thou shalt not live,
	That I may tell pale-hearted fear it lies,
	And sleep in spite of thunder. *Thunder.*

3rd Apparition appears, it is a child, crowned, with a tree in its hand.

Macbeth	What is this 90
	That rises like the issue of a king,
	And wears upon his baby-brow the round
	And top of sovereignty?
All Witches	Listen, but speak not to't.
3rd Apparition	Be lion-mettled, proud, and take no care
	Who chafes, who frets, or where conspirers are. 95
	Macbeth shall never vanquish'd be, until
	Great Birnam wood to high Dunsinane hill
	Shall come against him.

68 **farrow:** piglets
69 **sweaten:** sweated
69 **gibbet:** post that murders were hung from

72 **Thyself and office:** you and your role
72 **deftly:** skilfully

78 **harped:** guessed

80 **potent:** powerful

83 **resolute:** determined
84 **none:** no one

87 **make assurance double sure:** kill him anyway, to be on the safe side
88 **take a bond of fate:** make sure fate keeps its promise
89 **That I may:** so that I will be able to

91 **issue:** child
92–3 **round And top of sovereignty:** crown

94 **lion-mettled:** brave as a lion
95 **chafes:** argues, resists
95 **frets:** is unhappy with your reign
96 **vanquish'd:** defeated

Rachel Winters
Third Witch, spring 2010

In this scene, [and] I think right from the start of the play, they never actually have control over Macbeth, it's all about the power of suggestion. They suggest things, and OK so they tell him, this is going to happen to you, and he chooses to believe these things. They see this before this particular scene, and they see that he is going along with what they are saying, that he's tempted by it all. And when they meet him in this particular scene they know — well, he's already killed the king, he's killed Banquo, so they know they've got him. It's a funny one. [He comes in thinking he's in charge, but] he's the one who is asking all the questions and they choose to answer him, which shows, I think, that they are in control. At the end of the scene they are saying, 'seek to know no more'. Actually, we are not going to tell you any more. That's it. They are in control.

Janet Fullerlove
First Witch, summer 2010

When Macbeth comes in at the beginning of this scene, when we've been casting a spell and plotting, it is all very much part of our plan. We want Macbeth back. That's what the spell is all about. We start to cast, for us, the ultimate spell. This is the one where we want to get him, hook, line and sinker. We're calling him back almost. So when he comes in we're almost playing it as though we're surprised:, "Oh, it's you!" There is a point where he walks forward and says, "I want you to answer my questions". We're almost playing it with our back to him, as though we're going to not go there, and then we eventually say "Speak. Demand. We'll answer". That's when we think "Okay, now we've got him, we've really sucked him in here, he's coming all the way, we're going to take him right to the depths of this, he's going to be horrified by what we show him."

One of the supernatural events in Act 4 Scene 1.

1 Study the stage directions on pages 77 and 79. Which of them is shown in this photo?

2 What effect do you think Shakespeare was intending when he wrote this stage direction?

3rd Apparition descends.

Macbeth
                              That will never be.
Who can impress the forest, bid the tree
Unfix his earth-bound root? Sweet bodements, good!
Rebellious dead, rise never till the wood   100
Of Birnam rise, and our high-placed Macbeth
Shall live the lease of nature, pay his breath
To time and mortal custom. Yet my heart
Throbs to know one thing. Tell me, if your art   105
Can tell so much: shall Banquo's issue ever
Reign in this kingdom?

All Witches
                              Seek to know no more.

Macbeth
I will be satisfied. Deny me this,
And an eternal curse fall on you. Let me know —

The cauldron descends. Music (oboes) offstage.

Why sinks that cauldron? And what noise is this?   110

First Witch   Show.

Second Witch   Show.

Third Witch   Show.

All Witches
Show his eyes, and grieve his heart;
Come like shadows, so depart.   115

*A procession of eight kings, the last holding a mirror,
followed by the Ghost of Banquo. They move past Macbeth
during his next speech.*

Macbeth
Thou are too like the spirit of Banquo. Down!
Thy crown does sear mine eyeballs. And thy hair,
Thou other gold-bound brow, is like the first.
A third, is like the former. — Filthy hags!
Why do you show me this? — A fourth? Start, eyes!   120
What, will the line stretch out to th' crack of doom?
Another yet!? A seventh? I'll see no more.
And yet the eighth appears, who bears a glass
Which shows me many more. And some I see
That twofold balls and treble sceptres carry.   125
Horrible sight! Now I see 'tis true,
For the blood-boltered Banquo smiles upon me,
And points at them for his.

[The procession has left the stage.]

                              What? Is this so?

First Witch
Ay sir, all this is so. But why
Stands Macbeth thus amazedly?   130
Come sisters, cheer we up his sprites,
And show the best of our delights.
I'll charm the air to give a sound,
While you perform your antic round.
That this great king may kindly say,   135
Our duties did his welcome pay.

99	**impress:** force to join an army
100	**bodements:** predictions
101	**Rebellious dead:** Banquo
103–4	**the lease of nature … mortal custom:** his given life-span, dying naturally
105	**art:** skills
115	**so:** in the same way
117	**sear:** burn
118	**gold-bound brow:** crowned head
119	**former:** one before
120	**Start:** burst from your sockets
121	**th' crack of doom:** the Day of Judgement (when God sends the dead to Heaven or Hell)
125	**twofold balls … sceptres carry:** carrying the symbols of a ruler, but twice, to show he rules two countries, as King James ruled England and Scotland at the time
127	**blood-boltered:** smothered in blood
128	**for his:** as his descendants
130	**amazedly:** stunned
131	**sprites:** spirits
134	**antic round:** unnatural dance
136	**Our … pay:** we treated him respectfully and did as he asked

ACT 4 SCENE 1

Music. The Witches dance, then vanish.

Macbeth   Where are they? Gone? Let this pernicious hour
Stand aye accursèd in the calendar. —
Come in, without there!   *Enter Lennox.*

Lennox   What's your grace's will?

Macbeth   Saw you the weird sisters?

Lennox   No, my lord.   140

Macbeth   Came they not by you?

Lennox   No indeed, my lord.

Macbeth   Infected be the air whereon they ride,
And damned all those that trust them! — I did hear
The galloping of horse. Who was't came by?

Lennox   'Tis two or three, my lord, that bring you word.   145
Macduff is fled to England.

Macbeth   Fled to England?

Lennox   Ay, my good lord.

Macbeth   Time, thou anticipat'st my dread exploits.
The flighty purpose never is o'ertook   150
Unless the deed go with it. From this moment,
The very firstlings of my heart shall be
The firstlings of my hand. And even now
To crown my thoughts with acts, be it thought and done
The castle of Macduff I will surprise,   155
Seize upon Fife; give to th' edge o' th' sword
His wife, his babes, and all unfortunate souls
That trace him in his line. No boasting like a fool,
This deed I'll do, before this purpose cool.
But no more sights. — Where are these gentlemen?   160
Come bring me where they are.

Exit Macbeth and Lennox.

137 **pernicious:** dangerous
138 **aye:** forever
139 **Come in, without there!:** calling Lennox who is waiting outside
149 **anticipat'st:** have guessed
149 **dread exploits:** fearsome deeds
150–1 **The flighty ... with it:** Planning a deed isn't enough – you have to do it quickly
152–3 **The very firstlings ... hand:** From now on I must act as soon as I think of a deed
154 **crown:** follow through
155 **surprise:** attack without warning
156 **Fife:** the area Macduff rules
156 **give to ... sword:** kill
158 **trace him in his line:** are his descendants
159 **before this purpose cool:** at once
160 **sights:** visions

Director's Note, 4.1

✔ Macbeth visits the Witches.

✔ They show him visions which reassure him, but include 'beware Macduff'.

✔ He asks about Banquo, and is dismayed by a vision of many descendents of Banquo as kings.

✔ Shaken by this, and by the news that Macduff has fled, he decides to have Macduff's family killed.

✔ What effect do the visions have on Macbeth?

Text focus: Act 4 Scene 1 lines 129–161

(AO1) Response to characters and events:

- Macbeth cries of the weird sisters, "damned all those who trust them", yet because he continues to trust (selectively) in what they showed him, his belief in his invulnerability will betray him. *What clues do you find in his attitude and actions that he no longer needs prompting by his wife or by the Witches?*

- Macbeth once took comfort in the idea that "time and the hour runs through the roughest day", but time has enabled Macduff to flee, it will put Banquo's heirs on the throne and it will bring Macbeth to damnation. *Does Macbeth now see time as a friend or an enemy?*

- Macbeth said earlier that "words to the heat of deeds too cold breath gives" and now says, "be it thought and done". *Why does he want to remove the time between thought and deed?*

- Macbeth wants to kill without remorse as he did when a soldier, and starts by planning to kill Macduff's wife and children. *How might this influence the audience's attitude to Macbeth?*

(AO2) Language, structure and form:

- The very air is "infected" by the weird sisters, but also by Macbeth and his evil. *How does Shakespeare show that Macbeth is now the disease afflicting Scotland?*

- The word "crown" is a reminder to the audience that all his actions and sufferings are the result of seeking the crown of Scotland. *Is Shakespeare suggesting that he who holds the crown by treason, not by right, will not hold it for long?*

- Structurally this is a significant moment in the play. Shakespeare is showing the audience Macbeth as an evil tyrant. *How does he do this?*

- This is the last time the Witches appear on stage. *Are there any clues in their words that this might be so?*

(AO3) Context and ideas:

- Read the *Shakespeare's World* box on False Prophecies on page 104. *What would Shakespeare's original audiences have thought about the prophecies and Macbeth's reaction to them in this scene?*

- Sight, visions and appearance are major themes in the play. Macbeth did not dare to look again at Duncan's corpse and was rendered helpless by the sight of "blood-boltered Banquo", so now he wants "no more sights". *At this point in the play, which "sights" from earlier scenes are likely to be in the audience's mind?*

Question:

How do lines 135–161 contribute to Shakespeare's presentation of Macbeth as a tyrant?

Surrounded by the audience: an evening performance of *Macbeth*, summer 2010.

1 What impression of Lady Macduff and her family does this image give the audience?
2 How does Shakespeare's language influence our response to the family prior to their slaughter?

l–r (foreground) Mia Adams, Simone Kirby, Charlie George

ACT 4 SCENE 2

Enter Lady Macduff, her Son, and Ross.

Lady Macduff What had he done, to make him fly the land?

Ross You must have patience, madam.

Lady Macduff   He had none.
His flight was madness. When our actions do not,
Our fears do make us traitors.

3-4 When our actions … traitors: even the innocent can seem guilty if fear makes them run away

Ross   You know not
Whether it was his wisdom, or his fear.   5

Lady Macduff Wisdom? To leave his wife, to leave his babes,
His mansion and his titles, in a place
From whence himself does fly? He loves us not.
He wants the natural touch, for the poor wren,
The most diminutive of birds, will fight,   10
Her young ones in her nest, against the owl.
All is the fear, and nothing is the love;
As little is the wisdom, where the flight
So runs against all reason.

8 From whence: from which
9 wants the natural touch: lacks human feelings
10 most diminutive: smallest
12 All is the fear … love: his fear has overcome his love for his family
14 runs against all reason: makes no sense

Ross My dearest coz,   15
I pray you, school yourself. But for your husband,
He is noble, wise, judicious, and best knows
The fits o' th' season. I dare not speak much further,
But cruel are the times, when we are traitors
And do not know ourselves. When we hold rumour   20
From what we fear, yet know not what we fear,
But float upon a wild and violent sea
Each way and move. — I take my leave of you:
Shall not be long but I'll be here again.
Things at the worst will cease or else climb upward   25
To what they were before.   *[To the Son.]*

15 coz: cousin (used for close relative or friend)
16 school: control
18 fits o' th' season: violent changes of these times
20 And do not know ourselves: without realising it
20-1 hold rumour From what we fear: are driven by fear to believe rumours
23 Each way and move: tossed in all directions
25 climb upward: improve

                                        My pretty cousin,
Blessing upon you!

Lady Macduff Fathered he is, and yet he's fatherless.

Ross I am so much a fool, should I stay longer
It would be my disgrace and your discomfort.   30
I take my leave at once.   *Exit Ross.*

30 It would be … discomfort: I would embarrass us both by weeping
31 Sirrah: Boy

Lady Macduff   Sirrah, your father's dead,
And what will you do now? How will you live?

Son As birds do, mother.

Lady Macduff   What, with worms and flies?

Son With what I get, I mean, and so do they.

Lady Macduff Poor bird, thou'dst never fear the net, nor lime,   35
The pit-fall, nor the gin.

35-6 lime … pit-fall … gin: traps

Son Why should I, mother?
Poor birds they are not set for.
My father is not dead, for all your saying.

38 Poor birds … set for: they are only set for important people

ACT 4 SCENE 2

Lady Macduff	Yes, he is dead. How wilt thou do for father?	40
Son	Nay, how will you do for a husband?	
Lady Macduff	Why, I can buy me twenty at any market.	
Son	Then you'll buy 'em to sell again.	
Lady Macduff	Thou speak'st with all thy wit,	
	And yet, i' faith, with wit enough for thee.	45
Son	Was my father a traitor, mother?	
Lady Macduff	Ay, that he was.	
Son	What is a traitor?	
Lady Macduff	Why, one that swears and lies.	
Son	And be all traitors that do so?	50

44 **wit:** intelligence

49 **swears and lies:** makes a promise under oath and breaks it (but her son thinks she means ordinary swearing and lying)
50 **be all traitors ... so?:** are all who do that traitors?

Lady Macduff, the Murderers and her son in the background, spring 2010 production.

At what exact point in this scene was this photo taken? Quote directly from the text to support your answer.

Karen Bryson

exam SKILLS

Target skill: commenting on the impact of a key scene

Question: What impact does Shakespeare's presentation of Lady Macduff in lines 65–85 have on an audience?

Things you might talk about include:

- Why Shakespeare included this scene.
- Why he had the children on stage before introducing the murderers.
- Why Lady Macduff does not flee on hearing the messenger's warning.
- How the scene affects your view of Macbeth.

Now answer the question above.

Director's Note, 4.2

✔ Ross visits Lady Macduff. She cannot understand why Macduff has left his family in Scotland.
✔ We see a happy family, but they are interrupted, first by a warning, then by the Murderers.
✔ What effect does this scene have on the audience?

Lady Macduff   Everyone that does so is a traitor, and must be hanged.

Son   And must they all be hang'd that swear and lie?

Lady Macduff   Every one.

Son   Who must hang them?

Lady Macduff   Why, the honest men.   55

Son   Then the liars and swearers are fools. For there are liars
and swearers enough to beat the honest men and hang
up them.

Lady Macduff   Now God help thee, poor monkey. But how wilt thou
do for a father?   60

Son   If he were dead, you'd weep for him. If you would not,
it were a good sign that I should quickly have a new
father.

Lady Macduff   Poor prattler, how thou talk'st!   64 **prattler:** chatterbox

Enter Messenger.

Messenger   Bless you, fair dame. I am not to you known,   65
Though in your state of honor I am perfect.   66 **in your state … perfect:** I know
I doubt some danger does approach you nearly.   your status and reputation
If you will take a homely man's advice,   67 **doubt:** suspect
Be not found here. Hence with your little ones.   67 **nearly:** close by
To fright you thus, methinks I am too savage: 70 68 **homely:** simple, ordinary
To do worse to you were fell cruelty,   69 **Hence:** away from here
Which is too nigh your person. Heaven preserve you,   70–1 **To fright you … fell cruelty:**
I dare abide no longer.   *Exit Messenger.*   I'm sorry to scare you with this
                                                                           warning, but it would be even
                                                                           crueller not to warn you
                                                                      72 **nigh:** near
                                                                      73 **abide:** stay

Lady Macduff   Whither should I fly?
I have done no harm. But I remember now   75
I am in this earthly world: where to do harm
Is often laudable, to do good sometime   77 **laudable:** worthy of praise
Accounted dangerous folly. Why then, alas,   78 **Accounted:** considered to be
Do I put up that womanly defence,   78 **folly:** stupidity
To say I have done no harm?   *Enter Murderers.*

                         What are these faces?   80

Murderer   Where is your husband?

Lady Macduff   I hope in no place so unsanctified   82 **unsanctified:** unholy
Where such as thou may'st find him.

Murderer   He's a traitor.

Son   Thou liest, thou shag-eared villain!

Murderer   What, you egg?   *[Stabbing him.]*   84 **shag-eared:** with cut ears (some
Young fry of treachery!   crimes were punished by ear
                                                                       cutting)
Son   He has kill'd me, mother: 85   85 **Young fry of treachery!:** Son of
Run away, I pray you!   *[He dies.]*   a traitor!

*Exit Lady Macduff, crying "Murder", pursued by the
Murderers, one of whom takes the Son's body.*

WHAT I SAY AND WHAT I THINK

Malcolm is established in England and supported by "saintly" King Edward the Confessor, but fearful of attackers sent by Macbeth. The tension is palpable, although at the start of the scene neither man (unlike the audience) knows of the slaughter of Macduff's family.

Work in groups of four.

- Form two pairs and choose a section of around 20 lines from the Working Cut, or lines 215–34, or 235–55, checking that other groups have different passages to prepare.
- One pair plays Macduff, the other pair plays Malcolm.
- Within the pairs, decide who will speak and who will display.
- Prepare a presentation in which one of each pair is the character and says their words in the England scene, while behind them the other person displays a notice that shows what they are thinking, not what they are saying.
- Present the passages in sequence to an audience.

1 How is Malcolm presented in lines 27–60?
2 How is Macduff presented in lines 217–247?
3 How is Malcolm presented at the end of the scene?

Actor's view

Philip Cumbus
Malcolm, spring 2010

Malcolm has a wonderful self-awareness that I think the other characters do not have. I think by the virtue of the fact that he has imagined himself to be the worst king of all kings, the fact that he is aware enough to think that that is possible within himself, means that I think he'll be all right. I think he's got enough integrity and enough foresight to see where the bad path would lead so that that path can be avoided, as opposed to people like Macbeth. So I think Malcolm has enough foresight to be able to avoid some of the traps that were laid before him. So I think he might be all right.

Working Cut – text for experiment

Malc Let us seek out some desolate shade, and there
Weep our sad bosoms empty.
This tyrant, whose sole name blisters our tongues,
Was once thought honest. You have loved him well.

Macd I am not treacherous.

Malc But Macbeth is.
That which you are, my thoughts cannot transpose.
Angels are bright still, though the brightest fell.
Why in that rawness left you wife and child,
Without leave-taking?

Macd Bleed, bleed, poor country!
The title is affeerrd. Fare thee well, lord,
I would not be the villain that thou think'st.

Malc Be not offended.
When I shall tread upon the tyrant's head,
Or wear it on my sword, yet my poor country
Shall have more vices than it had before;
More suffer, and more sundry ways than ever,
By him that shall succeed.

Macd What should he be?

Malc It is myself I mean, in whom I know
All the particulars of vice so grafted,
That when they shall be opened, black Macbeth
Will seem as pure as snow, and the poor state
Esteem him as a lamb, being compared
With my confineless harms.

Macd Not in the legions
Of horrid hell can come a devil more damned
In evils to top Macbeth.

Malc I grant him bloody,
Luxurious, avaricious, false, deceitful,
Sudden, malicious, smacking of every sin
That has a name. But there's no bottom, none,
In my voluptuousness. Your wives, your daughters,
Your matrons, and your maids, could not fill up
The cistern of my lust. Better Macbeth
Than such an one to reign.

Macd O Scotland, Scotland!

Malc If such a one be fit to govern, speak.
I am as I have spoken.

Macd Fit to govern?
No, not to live. O nation miserable!
These evils thou repeat'st upon thyself
Have banished me from Scotland. O my breast,
Thy hope ends here!

Malc Macduff, this noble passion,
Child of integrity, hath from my soul
Wiped the black scruples, reconciled my thoughts
To thy good truth and honour. I am yet
Unknown to woman, never was forsworn,
Scarcely have coveted what was mine own,
My first false speaking was this upon myself.
What I am truly is my poor country's to command.

Enter Malcolm and Macduff.

Malcolm	Let us seek out some desolate shade, and there Weep our sad bosoms empty.
Macduff	Let us rather Hold fast the mortal sword, and like good men, Bestride our downfall'n birthdom. Each new morn
	New widows howl, new orphans cry, new sorrows Strike heaven on the face, that it resounds As if it felt with Scotland, and yelled out Like syllable of dolour.
Malcolm	What I believe, I'll wail;
	What know, believe; and what I can redress, As I shall find the time to friend, I will. What you have spoke, it may be so perchance. This tyrant, whose sole name blisters our tongues, Was once thought honest. You have loved him well,
	He hath not touched you yet. I am young, but something You may discern of him through me, and wisdom To offer up a weak, poor innocent lamb To appease an angry god.
Macduff	I am not treacherous.
Malcolm	But Macbeth is.
	A good and virtuous nature may recoil In an imperial charge. But I shall crave your pardon. That which you are, my thoughts cannot transpose. Angels are bright still, though the brightest fell.
	Though all things foul would wear the brows of grace, Yet grace must still look so.
Macduff	I have lost my hopes.
Malcolm	Perchance even there where I did find my doubts. Why in that rawness left you wife and child, (Those precious motives, those strong knots of love),
	Without leave-taking? I pray you, Let not my jealousies be your dishonours, But mine own safeties. You may be rightly just, Whatever I shall think.
Macduff	Bleed, bleed, poor country!
	Great tyranny, lay thou thy basis sure, For goodness dare not check thee. Wear thou thy wrongs, The title is affeerrd. Fare thee well, lord, I would not be the villain that thou think'st
	For the whole space that's in the tyrant's grasp And the rich East to boot.
Malcolm	Be not offended. I speak not as in absolute fear of you. I think our country sinks beneath the yoke, It weeps, it bleeds, and each new day a gash

Line numbers: 5, 10, 15, 20, 25, 30, 35, 40, 45

1 **desolate shade:** lonely place

4 **fast:** tightly
4 **mortal:** deadly
5 **Bestride our downfall'n birthdom:** defend the fallen country of our birth
7 **that:** so that
9 **Like syllable of dolour:** the same miserable cries
10 **wail:** weep over
11 **redress:** put right
12 **As I shall ... will:** At the most favourable time
13 **perchance:** perhaps
14 **sole name:** name alone
16-7 **something You may ... through me:** you might see the difference between us
18-9 **To offer up ... god:** to hand me over to him to keep him happy
21-2 **recoil In an imperial charge:** give way to a king's demands
23 **transpose:** change into something else
24 **the brightest fell:** the brightest angel, Lucifer, rebelled and became the Devil
25-6 **Though all things foul ... look so:** Evil people try to seem good, but don't forget that those who are good also seem good
29 **in that rawness:** unprotected
30 **motives:** reasons for doing things
31 **leave-taking:** permission to go from the king
32 **jealousies be your dishonours:** suspicions seem to suggest you are dishonourable
33 **But mine own safeties:** I'm concerned for my own safety
33 **rightly just:** completely honest
36-7 **lay thou ... check thee:** you can get a strong grip on the country, when good people don't dare to stop you
37-8 **Wear thou ... title is affeerrd:** You don't need to hide your evil deeds, your claim to the throne is confirmed
40 **the whole space:** all the land (Scotland)
41 **to boot:** too
44 **sinks beneath the yoke:** is dragged down by Macbeth's tyranny

Malcolm and Macduff, spring 2010.

There is no stage direction that Macduff should draw his sword on Malcolm. What justification is there in lines 99–124 for staging a moment in the scene in this way?

Philip Cumbus, Nicholas Khan

Is added to her wounds. I think withal There would be hands uplifted in my right, And here from gracious England have I offer Of goodly thousands. But, for all this, When I shall tread upon the tyrant's head, 50 Or wear it on my sword, yet my poor country Shall have more vices than it had before; More suffer, and more sundry ways than ever, By him that shall succeed.	**46 withal:** also **47 hands uplifted … right:** people willing to fight to make me king of Scotland **48 gracious England:** the English king **51 wear it on my sword:** cut it off and show it on the end of my sword **53 more sundry ways:** in different ways

Macduff   What should he be?

54 What should he be?: who do you mean?

Malcolm   It is myself I mean, in whom I know   55
All the particulars of vice so grafted,
That when they shall be opened, black Macbeth
Will seem as pure as snow, and the poor state
Esteem him as a lamb, being compared
With my confineless harms.   60

56-7 All the particulars … be opened: have so many vices that when you know them

59 Esteem: value

60 confineless harms: limitless evils

Macduff   Not in the legions
Of horrid hell can come a devil more damned
In evils to top Macbeth.

61 legions: armies

63 top: go further than

Malcolm   I grant him bloody,
Luxurious, avaricious, false, deceitful,   65
Sudden, malicious, smacking of every sin
That has a name. But there's no bottom, none,

65 Luxurious: lustful
65 avaricious: greedy for wealth
66 Sudden: unpredictable
66 smacking of: touched by

In my voluptuousness. Your wives, your daughters,
Your matrons, and your maids, could not fill up
The cistern of my lust, and my desire   70
All continent impediments would o'erbear,
That did oppose my will. Better Macbeth
Than such an one to reign.

Macduff
Boundless intemperance
In nature is a tyranny. It hath been   75
Th' untimely emptying of the happy throne,
And fall of many kings. But fear not yet
To take upon you what is yours. You may
Convey your pleasures in a spacious plenty,
And yet seem cold. The time you may so hoodwink.   80
We have willing dames enough. There cannot be
That vulture in you, to devour so many
As will to greatness dedicate themselves,
Finding it so inclined.

Malcolm
With this, there grows
In my most ill-composed affection, such   85
A staunchless avarice, that were I king,
I should cut off the nobles for their lands.
Desire his jewels, and this other's house,
And my more-having would be as a sauce
To make me hunger more, that I should forge   90
Quarrels unjust against the good and loyal,
Destroying them for wealth.

Macduff
This avarice
Sticks deeper; grows with more pernicious root
Than summer-seeming lust, and it hath been
The sword of our slain kings. Yet do not fear;   95
Scotland hath foisons to fill up your will
Of your mere own. All these are portable,
With other graces weighed.

Malcolm
But I have none. The king-becoming graces,
As justice, verity, temp'rance, stableness,   100
Bounty, perseverance, mercy, lowliness,
Devotion, patience, courage, fortitude,
I have no relish of them, but abound
In the division of each several crime,
Acting it many ways. Nay, had I power, I should   105
Pour the sweet milk of concord into hell,
Uproar the universal peace, confound
All unity on earth.

Macduff
O Scotland, Scotland!

Malcolm
If such a one be fit to govern, speak.   110
I am as I have spoken.

Macduff
Fit to govern?
No, not to live. O nation miserable!
With an untitled tyrant bloody-sceptered,
When shalt thou see thy wholesome days again?   115
Since that the truest issue of thy throne

68 **voluptuousness:** desire for pleasure
69 **matrons:** older (usually married) women
70 **fill up ... lust:** satisfy me
71 **All continent ... o'erbear:** would force anyone

74 **Boundless intemperance:** wild lack of self-control
76 **Th' ... throne:** the cause of many a king losing his throne
79–80 **Convey your pleasures ... hoodwink:** take your pleasure secretly, tricking people into thinking you are pure

83-4 **As will to ... inclined:** as would happily sleep with a king if he wanted it
85 **ill-composed affection:** evil nature
86 **staunchless avarice:** unstoppable greed
87 **cut off:** kill
89–90 **my more-having ... more:** the more I took, the more I would want
90 **that:** so that
90 **forge:** make, invent
93-4 **more ... summer-seeming lust:** more deeply-rooted, harder to stop than youthful
95 **sword of our slain kings:** caused the death on many kings
96 **foisons:** enough wealth
97 **Of your mere own:** just from your royal possessions
97 **these:** these vices
97 **portable:** bearable
98 **With other graces weighed:** set against your good points
99 **king-becoming graces:** virtues a king should have
100 **As:** such as
100 **verity:** truthfulness
100 **temp'rance:** self-restraint
101 **Bounty:** generosity
101 **lowliness:** humility, lack of pride
102 **Devotion:** love of God
102 **fortitude:** endurance
103 **relish:** taste for, enjoyment of
103-5 **abound In the division ... many ways:** enjoy committing sin in many different ways
106 **concord:** peace, harmony
107 **Uproar:** throw into confusion
107 **confound:** disrupt
114 **untitled:** with no right to rule
115 **wholesome:** healthy
116 **truest issue of thy throne:** person with most right to be king

89

By his own interdiction stands accursed
And does blaspheme his breed? Thy royal father
Was a most sainted king. The queen that bore thee,
Oft'ner upon her knees than on her feet,
Died every day she lived. Fare thee well.   120
These evils thou repeat'st upon thyself
Have banished me from Scotland. O my breast,
Thy hope ends here!

Malcolm   Macduff, this noble passion,   125
Child of integrity, hath from my soul
Wiped the black scruples, reconciled my thoughts
To thy good truth and honour. Devilish Macbeth,
By many of these trains, hath sought to win me
Into his power, and modest wisdom plucks me   130
From over-credulous haste. But God above
Deal between thee and me. For even now
I put myself to thy direction, and
Unspeak mine own detraction. Here abjure
The taints and blames I laid upon myself,   135
For strangers to my nature. I am yet
Unknown to woman, never was forsworn,
Scarcely have coveted what was mine own,
At no time broke my faith, would not betray
The devil to his fellow, and delight   140
No less in truth than life. My first false speaking
Was this upon myself. What I am truly
Is thine and my poor country's to command.
Whither, indeed, before thy here-approach,
Old Siward with ten thousand warlike men   145
Already at a point, was setting forth.
Now we'll together; and the chance of goodness
Be like our warranted quarrel. Why are you silent?

Macduff   Such welcome and unwelcome things at once   150

Enter a Doctor.

'Tis hard to reconcile. Well, more anon. —
Comes the king forth, I pray you?

Doctor   Ay, sir. There are a crew of wretched souls
That stay his cure. Their malady convinces
The great assay of art. But at his touch,
Such sanctity hath heaven given his hand,   155
They presently amend.

Malcolm   I thank you, doctor.   *Exit Doctor.*

Macduff   What's the disease he means?

Malcolm   'Tis called the evil.
A most miraculous work in this good king,   160
Which often, since my here-remain in England,
I have seen him do. How he solicits heaven
Himself best knows, but strangely-visited people
All swoll'n and ulcerous, pitiful to the eye,
The mere despair of surgery, he cures,   165

---

117 **interdiction:** accusation
118 **does blaspheme his breed:** dishonours his family
121 **Died every day she lived:** daily prayed for forgiveness to be sure of going to heaven when she died
122-3 **These evils ... Scotland:** your confession has destroyed any hope I had of returning to Scotland
126 **Child of integrity:** born of your honest nature
127 **black scruples:** sinister doubts
127-8 **reconciled my thoughts ... truth and honour:** convinced me you are honest
129 **by many of these trains:** sending people to say what Macduff has said to Malcolm to trick him into going back to Scotland
130-1 **modest wisdom ... haste:** I have to be careful who I believe
133 **to thy direction:** in your hands
134 **Unspeak mine own detraction:** take back my accusations against myself
134 **abjure:** deny
135 **taints and blames ... myself:** sins I accused myself of
136 **For strangers to my nature:** as totally unlike me
137 **Unknown to woman:** a virgin
137 **was forsworn:** broke an oath
138 **Scarcely have coveted ... own:** have hardly even desired my own possessions
139 **my faith:** a solemn promise
141 **false speaking:** lie
144 **Whither:** Where (to Scotland)
144 **here-approach:** arrival here
146 **at a point:** ready for battle
147-8 **chance of goodness ... quarrel:** may we be as successful as our reason for fighting is right
150 **Such welcome ... reconcile:** I have heard two such different stories – one welcome, the other not – that it is hard to know what to think
153 **stay his cure:** wait for him to cure them
153-6 **Their malady ... amend:** They have a disease that they believe God has given him the power to cure by touch
159 **the evil:** scrofula
161 **here-remain:** stay here
162 **solicits:** gets help from
163 **strangely-visited:** those with the disease

Hanging a golden stamp about their necks,
Put on with holy prayers. And 'tis spoken,
To the succeeding royalty he leaves
The healing benediction. With this strange virtue,
He hath a heavenly gift of prophecy,
And sundry blessings hang about his throne,
That speak him full of grace.

Enter Ross.

Macduff	See, who comes here?
Malcolm	My countryman, but yet I know him not.
Macduff	My ever-gentle cousin, welcome hither.
Malcolm	I know him now. Good God betimes remove The means that makes us strangers.
Ross	Sir, amen
Macduff	Stands Scotland where it did?
Ross	Alas poor country, Almost afraid to know itself. It cannot Be called our mother, but our grave, where nothing But who knows nothing, is once seen to smile. Where sighs and groans and shrieks that rent the air Are made, not marked. Where violent sorrow seems A modern ecstasy. The dead man's knell Is there scarce asked for who, and good men's lives Expire before the flowers in their caps, Dying or ere they sicken.
Macduff	O relation Too nice, and yet too true!
Malcolm	What's the newest grief?
Ross	That of an hour's age doth hiss the speaker,

166 **stamp:** coin
167 **Put on with holy prayers:** which he has prayed over
168–9 **To the succeeding ... benediction:** his descendants will inherit this power
170

173 **but ... not:** but I don't recognise him

175
176 **The means ... strangers:** the separation that makes strangers of us
177 **Stands ... did?:** Is the situation in Scotland unchanged?
180–1 **nothing ... to smile:** where only those who don't know what is going on can be cheerful
180
182 **rent:** tear, split
183 **Are ... marked:** are not even commented on
184 **modern ecstasy:** everyday emotion
184–5 **The ... who:** people hardly bother to ask who the funeral bell is ringing for
185
186 **Expire:** die, end
187 **or ere they sicken:** before
188 **O relation ... true:** The details of this account are awful, but, sadly, all too accurate
189 **nice:** accurate
190
191 **That of an hour's ... speaker:** what happened an hour ago is old news

SHAKESPEARE'S WORLD

THE KING'S EVIL

We call this disease scrofula, but in Shakespeare's time it was called *the King's Evil*, because many people believed it could be cured by being touched by the monarch. People believed Edward the Confessor started the practice of 'touching' sufferers. Historically he was king of England when Macbeth was king of Scotland. The practice had died out during the Middle Ages, but Mary Tudor revived it, and Queen Elizabeth, and then James I, continued the practice. James believed he was king by *divine right* (God's will) and that God was healing the sick through the special person of his anointed king.

exam SKILLS

Target skill: exploring the presentation of ideas

Question: How are the ideas of good and evil presented in Act 4 Scene 3?

Following the killing of Duncan, evil has been shown overtaking Scotland during the reign of "devilish Macbeth". Malcolm, representing good, is linked with the "grace" of English King Edward. Consider:

• The description of Scotland as a country "almost afraid to know itself".
• The words in this scene which link Malcolm with heaven and goodness.
• Why Edward the Confessor's power to overcome "the evil" were mentioned.

	Each minute teems a new one.
Macduff	How does my wife?
Ross	Why well.
Macduff	And all my children?
Ross	Well too.
Macduff	The tyrant has not battered at their peace?
Ross	No, they were well at peace, when I did leave 'em.
Macduff	Be not a niggard of your speech. How goes't?
Ross	When I came hither to transport the tidings,
	Which I have heavily borne, there ran a rumour
	Of many worthy fellows that were out,
	Which was to my belief witnessed the rather,
	For that I saw the tyrant's power a-foot.
	Now is the time of help. Your eye in Scotland
	Would create soldiers, make our women fight,
	To doff their dire distresses.
Malcolm	Be't their comfort
	We are coming thither. Gracious England hath
	Lent us good Siward and ten thousand men,
	An older and a better soldier none
	That Christendom gives out.
Ross	Would I could answer
	This comfort with the like. But I have words
	That would be howled out in the desert air,
	Where hearing should not latch them.
Macduff	What concern they?
	The general cause? Or is it a fee-grief
	Due to some single breast?
Ross	No mind that's honest
	But in it shares some woe, though the main part
	Pertains to you alone.
Macduff	If it be mine,
	Keep it not from me, quickly let me have it.
Ross	Let not your ears despise my tongue for ever,
	Which shall possess them with the heaviest sound
	That ever yet they heard.
Macduff	H'm: I guess at it.
Ross	Your castle is surprised. Your wife and babes
	Savagely slaughtered. To relate the manner
	Were, on the quarry of these murdered deer
	To add the death of you.
Malcolm	Merciful heaven!
	What, man, ne'er pull your hat upon your brows.
	Give sorrow words. The grief that does not speak
	Whispers the o'er-fraught heart and bids it break.

192 **teems a new one:** is filled with new examples

195

199 **Be not a niggard ... speech:** tell the whole story
200 200 **tidings:** news
201 **heavily borne:** have found hard to bear
202 **out:** prepared for battle
203–4 **to my belief ... a-foot:** I was ready to believe because Macbeth's army was on the march
205 205 **eye:** arrival, being seen
207 **doff their dire distresses:** get rid of their miseries (Macbeth's rule)

210 210–1 **An older ... out:** There's no better soldier in the whole Christian world
212 **Would:** I wish
213 **the like:** equally cheering news

215 215 **latch:** catch

217 **The general cause:** the fate of Scotland
217–8 **fee-grief ... breast:** bad news for just one person
219–20 **No mind that's ... some woe:** any honest person shares the trouble
220

221 **Pertains:** belongs

224 **possess:** tell
225

227 **is surprised:** has been attacked without warning
228–30 **To relate ... you:** If I were to tell you how, it would kill you too
230

232 **ne'er pull ... brows:** don't hide your face

234 **Whispers the o'er-fraught:** whispers to the over-loaded

Macduff	My children too?	235
Ross	Wife, children, servants, all that could be found.	
Macduff	And I must be from thence? My wife killed too?	
Ross	I have said.	
Malcolm	Be comforted. Let's make us med'cines of our great revenge, To cure this deadly grief.	240
Macduff	He has no children. — All my pretty ones? Did you say all? — O hell-kite! — All? What, all my pretty chickens and their dam At one fell swoop?	
Malcolm	Dispute it like a man.	245
Macduff	I shall do so. But I must also feel it as a man. I cannot but remember such things were That were most precious to me. Did heaven look on, And would not take their part? Sinful Macduff, They were all struck for thee! Naught that I am, Not for their own demerits, but for mine, Fell slaughter on their souls. Heaven rest them now.	250
Malcolm	Be this the whetstone of your sword. Let grief Convert to anger. Blunt not the heart, enrage it.	255
Macduff	O, I could play the woman with mine eyes And braggart with my tongue. — But gentle heavens, Cut short all intermission. Front to front Bring thou this fiend of Scotland and myself. Within my sword's length set him, if he 'scape, Heaven forgive him too.	260
Malcolm	This tune goes manly. Come, go we to the king, our power is ready, Our lack is nothing but our leave. Macbeth Is ripe for shaking, and the powers above Put on their instruments. Receive what cheer you may, The night is long, that never finds the day.	265

Exit all.

244 dam: mother

245 fell: deadly
245 Dispute: Deal with

250 take their part: act to save them
251 Naught that: worthless as
252 demerits: faults, failings
254 whetstone: a tool used to sharpen blades
255 Blunt not the heart: don't shut down your feelings
256 play the woman ... eyes: weep
257 braggart with my tongue: boast of the revenge I'll take
258 Cut short all intermission: don't leave time for that
258 Front to front: face to face
262 tune goes: way of speaking is
263 power: army
264 Our lack is ... leave: All we have left to do is say farewell to King Edward
265 ripe for shaking: at a point where he can be pushed from the throne
266 Put on their instruments: are getting ready too

Director's Note, 4.3

✔ Macduff joins Malcolm in England. At first Malcolm thinks this might be a plot to betray him to Macbeth.

✔ Malcolm decides to trust Macduff, and tells him he has an English army ready to invade Scotland.

✔ Ross arrives with news from Scotland. He tells Macduff his family has been murdered.

✔ What impression of Macbeth as a king do we get in this scene?

A

C

Lady Macbeth, the sleepwalking scene.

1 How does Shakespeare use Lady Macbeth's language to show her state of mind? Quote directly from the text to support your answer.

2 How are the actors in the photos trying to show her state of mind?

A: summer 2010, Laura Rogers; B: 2001, Eve Best; C: 2013, Samantha Spiro

B

SHAKESPEARE'S WORLD
◇◇◇◇◇◇◇◇◇◇◇◇

The Waiting Gentlewoman

In Shakespeare's day, the Queen's waiting gentlewomen were members of the court. They came from noble families, often with strong royal connections. Although she was a servant, a gentlewoman did not clean or cook for the family. She was a companion. She might read to, or play music for her mistress. At times, a waiting woman might even advise her mistress on the latest dress, dances and music fashionable at the time. Waiting women often knew family secrets, since they lived in close quarters with the family, as does Lady Macbeth's gentlewoman in this scene.

ACT 5 SCENE 1

Enter a Doctor of Physic and a Waiting-Gentlewoman.

Doctor I have two nights watched with you, but can perceive no truth in your report. When was it she last walked?

Gentlewoman Since his majesty went into the field, I have seen her rise from her bed, throw her nightgown upon her, unlock her closet, take forth paper, fold it, write upon't, read it, afterwards seal it, and again return to bed; yet all this while in a most fast sleep.

Doctor A great perturbation in nature, to receive at once the benefit of sleep, and do the effects of watching. In this slumbery agitation, besides her walking and other actual performances, what (at any time) have you heard her say?

Gentlewoman That, sir, which I will not report after her.

Doctor You may to me, and 'tis most meet you should.

Gentlewoman Neither to you, nor any one, having no witness to confirm my speech.

Enter Lady Macbeth, in her nightgown, with a candle.

Lo you, here she comes. This is her very guise, and upon my life, fast asleep. Observe her, stand close.

Doctor How came she by that light?

Gentlewoman Why it stood by her. She has light by her continually, 'tis her command.

Doctor You see her eyes are open.

Gentlewoman Ay but their sense are shut.

Doctor What is it she does now?
Look how she rubs her hands.

Gentlewoman It is an accustomed action with her, to seem thus washing her hands. I have known her continue in this a quarter of an hour.

Lady Macbeth Yet here's a spot.

Doctor Hark, she speaks. I will set down what comes from her, to satisfy my remembrance the more strongly.

Lady Macbeth Out damned spot! Out I say! One: Two: why then 'tis time to do't. Hell is murky. Fie, my lord, fie, a soldier, and afeard? What need we fear? Who knows it, when none can call our power to account? Yet who would have thought the old man to have had so much blood in him?

Doctor Do you mark that?

Lady Macbeth The Thane of Fife, had a wife: where is she now? What, will these hands ne'er be clean? No more o' that my lord, no more o' that. You mar all with this starting.

---

3 **went into the field:** led his army off to fight the rebels

5 **closet:** private storage box

8 **perturbation in nature:** disturbance of her normal state of mind

8 **at once:** at the same time

9 **do the effects of watching:** act as if awake

10 **slumbery agitation:** sleepwalking

11 **actual performances:** things you have actually seen her do

13 **report after her:** repeat

14 **meet:** suitable, right

17 **her very guise:** the way she behaved before

18 **stand close:** don't let her see you

23 **their sense are shut:** they don't see

26 **accustomed:** usual (when she sleepwalks)

30 **set:** write

31 **to satisfy my ... strongly:** so I will remember it more accurately

32 **One: Two:** counting the striking of a bell

35 **none can call ... account:** we'll be so powerful no one can accuse us

38 **mark:** hear

39 **Thane of Fife:** Macduff

41 **You mar all ... starting:** Your nervous behaviour will ruin everything

95

Laura Rogers
Lady Macbeth, summer 2010

[This scene] is a challenge in itself, purely because, from an actor's point of view, you have been off stage for such a long time – the last thing they see of you is the banquet scene.

Before the sleep-walking scene you've had huge sleep deprivation, so you feel that you're going slightly insane as well and because when you do sleep you just have these images in your head. So, it's a brilliant scene for an actress to play because it does allow you to play it in any way you like because people react to madness differently. It felt very freeing. Obviously, you know, I don't suffer from sleep-walking myself and I'm not aware of anyone that does. So, you just have to put yourself in that position. It's written so well for you. The challenge, I suppose, is, like any challenge at the Globe, that you can see the audience. And so you have to just imagine that there's nobody there, and how you would behave if you thought there was nobody witnessing it. But, I think, for me that was one of my favourite scenes. Once you get yourself into that place, then there's nothing you can't do with that scene. And the director and I talked about it. I suppose it could be played incredibly manic, but she [Lucy Bailey, the director] said that she wanted the audience to really sympathise with the character at this point, and just see the scared little girl come out. That she's done this terrible thing but [she] does regret; she can never go back and take that moment back. And what's it's doing to her mind. [Lucy] wanted to see somebody that almost died from the inside. And so, hopefully, the audience did.

FROM THE REHEARSAL ROOM...

LADY MACBETH

- Work in pairs.
- In this scene, Lady Macbeth refers to past events. Decide what events she is referring to, and find the scenes in the play where these events take place.

1 Sit back-to-back while one person chooses and reads out words and phrases from the original event and the other then reads out the relevant words from Act 5 Scene 1.

2 The audience sees a different side to Lady Macbeth in this scene. What has happened to her state of mind since the end of the banquet, and why? Quote from the text to support your answer.

exam PREPARATION

Text focus: Act 5 Scene 1 lines 29–63

Lady Macbeth has not been on stage since the end of the banquet scene, but Shakespeare uses the opening conversation between the Doctor and the gentlewoman to warn the audience to expect a changed woman, walking and talking in her sleep and afflicted by a "great perturbation in nature".

(AO1) Response to characters and events:
- In a complete reversal of her behaviour Lady Macbeth now fears the darkness she once craved: the candle is by her continually. *How might audiences respond to her need for light?*
- Good answers take evidence from different points in the play as support. Commenting on this extract you should refer back to something Lady Macbeth says (twice) in Act 2 Scene 2. *What?*
- Earlier in the play, Lady Macbeth was strong enough to deny her own feminine instincts for Macbeth's sake, but she now pays the price when her unconscious mind is undermined by guilt. *Do we feel any sympathy for her at this point?*
- Her words recall, in fractured form, the past crimes of the couple, when they were a couple. She went from being Macbeth's "dearest partner of greatness" to someone who was kept "innocent of the knowledge" of

Macbeth's later crimes. *What evidence has there been of the growing gulf between husband and wife?*

(AO2) Language, structure and form:
- The broken rhythms and dislocation of Lady Macbeth's speech, full of exclamations and questioning, reflect her deep distress. *Does her language suggest that her mind is dislocated too?*
- The visceral power of the word "smell" has a physicality that makes the blood almost tangible. When she says, "Who would have thought the old man to have had so much blood in him", we are reminded of her earlier thought that "had he not resembled my father as he slept, I had done it". *How conscious has Lady Macbeth been all along that she needed to control and crush her humanity?*

(AO3) Context and ideas:
- Lady Macbeth's actions were more real than the unreal images escaping in sleep from her unconscious mind. *Is Shakespeare showing the inner world of a human being as linked with the outer world of society?*
- Justice, human and divine, is one theme of the play. *Is Lady Macbeth's suffering evidence that "we still have judgement here"?*

Question:
How does Shakespeare present Lady Macbeth as disturbed in lines 29–63?

Doctor	Go to, go to. You have known what you should not.
Gentlewoman	She has spoke what she should not, I am sure of that. Heaven knows what she has known. 45
Lady Macbeth	Here's the smell of the blood still. All the perfumes of Arabia will not sweeten this little hand. Oh, oh, oh!
Doctor	What a sigh is there! The heart is sorely charged.
Gentlewoman	I would not have such a heart in my bosom for the 50 dignity of the whole body.
Doctor	Well, well, well.
Gentlewoman	Pray God it be, sir.
Doctor	This disease is beyond my practice. Yet I have known those which have walked in their sleep, who have died 55 holily in their beds.
Lady Macbeth	Wash your hands, put on your nightgown, look not so pale. I tell you yet again Banquo's buried; he cannot come out on's grave.
Doctor	Even so? 60
Lady Macbeth	To bed, to bed. There's knocking at the gate. Come, come, come, come, give me your hand. What's done, cannot be undone. To bed, to bed, to bed.

Exit Lady Macbeth.

Doctor	Will she go now to bed?
Gentlewoman	Directly. 65
Doctor	Foul whisperings are abroad. Unnatural deeds Do breed unnatural troubles. Infected minds To their deaf pillows will discharge their secrets. More needs she the divine than the physician. God, God, forgive us all. Look after her, 70 Remove from her the means of all annoyance, And still keep eyes upon her. So, good-night, My mind she has mated, and amazed my sight. I think, but dare not speak.
Gentlewoman	Good-night, good doctor. *They exit.* 75

ACT 5 SCENE 2

Enter soldiers: a drummer, and others with flags. Then enter Menteith, Caithness, Angus, Lennox, and more Soldiers.

Menteith	The English power is near, led on by Malcolm, His uncle Siward, and the good Macduff. Revenges burn in them, for their dear causes Would to the bleeding and the grim alarm Excite the mortified man. 5

49 **sorely charged:** weighed down with grief

51 **dignity of the whole body:** position of queen

54 **beyond my practice:** too difficult for my skills to cure

55–6 **who have died ... beds:** and it has not killed them

59 **on's:** of his

60 **Even so?:** So that's it?

65 **Directly:** straight away
66 **Foul whisperings are abroad:** terrible rumours are spreading
69 **divine:** priest (to confess her sins to)
71 **the means of all annoyance:** anything she could harm herself with
73 **mated:** bewildered

Director's Note, 5.1

✔ Lady Macbeth is watched as she sleepwalks by her Gentlewoman and a Doctor.

✔ She seems to wash her hands, and talks about the murders she has been involved in.

✔ What they have heard scares the Gentlewoman and Doctor.

3 **their dear causes:** the wrongs they are revenging
4–5 **to the bleeding ... man:** rouse even a dead man to fight for them

97

Macbeth, centre, and two attendants, 2013 production.

At which point at the start of Act 5 Scene 3 was this photo taken? Quote directly from the text to support your answer.

Ed Pinker, Joseph Millson, Mark Borthwick

FROM THE REHEARSAL ROOM...

REPORTS ABOUT MACBETH

- In groups of four, read through Act 5 Scene 2.
- List the words and phrases that the Scottish lords use to describe Macbeth.

1 What information are we given in this scene?

2 What is the impact of the images used to describe Macbeth?

3 Why might Shakespeare have chosen to show us Macbeth through the eyes of Scottish lords at this point in the play?

exam SKILLS

Target skill: analysing structure and language

Question: How does the presentation of Macbeth in lines 1–30 influence our attitude to him?

- Shakespeare reminds us of the Witches' predictions through Macbeth's speech, although the audience don't yet know how his faith in the predictions will betray him.
- In pairs, look back at exactly what the apparitions said and work out what Macbeth has remembered and forgotten.
- How far does Macbeth's desperate courage depend on his faith in the predictions?
- Macbeth sounds old before his time. Which images carry his regret most poignantly?

Angus	Near Birnam Wood
	Shall we well meet them, that way are they coming.
Caithness	Who knows if Donalbain be with his brother?
Lennox	For certain, sir, he is not. I have a file
	Of all the gentry; there is Siward's son 10
	And many unrough youths, that even now
	Protest their first of manhood.
Menteith	What does the tyrant?
Caithness	Great Dunsinane he strongly fortifies.
	Some say he's mad. Others, that lesser hate him, 15
	Do call it valiant fury, but for certain
	He cannot buckle his distempered cause
	Within the belt of rule.
Angus	Now does he feel
	His secret murders sticking on his hands,
	Now minutely revolts upbraid his faith-breach. 20
	Those he commands move only in command,
	Nothing in love. Now does he feel his title
	Hang loose about him, like a giant's robe
	Upon a dwarfish thief.
Menteith	Who then shall blame
	His pestered senses to recoil and start, 25
	When all that is within him does condemn
	Itself for being there?
Caithness	Well, march we on,
	To give obedience where 'tis truly owed.
	Meet we the med'cine of the sickly weal,
	And with him pour we in our country's purge, 30
	Each drop of us.
Lennox	Or so much as it needs,
	To dew the sovereign flower, and drown the weeds.
	Make we our march towards Birnam. *Exit all, marching.*

ACT 5 SCENE 3

Enter Macbeth, Doctor, and Attendants.

Macbeth	Bring me no more reports, let them fly all.
	Till Birnam Wood remove to Dunsinane,
	I cannot taint with fear. What's the boy Malcolm?
	Was he not born of woman? The spirits that know
	All mortal consequences have pronounced me thus: 5
	"Fear not, Macbeth, no man that's born of woman
	Shall e'er have power upon thee." Then fly, false thanes,
	And mingle with the English epicures.
	The mind I sway by, and the heart I bear,
	Shall never sag with doubt, nor shake with fear. 10

Enter a Servant.

The devil damn thee black, thou cream-faced loon!
Where got'st thou that goose look?

7 **well:** have the advantage if we
9 **file:** list
10 **gentry:** people of good birth (in the army)
11-2 **unrough youths ... manhood:** young men in battle for the first time
15 **lesser hate him:** don't hate him as much
16 **valiant fury:** warlike rage
17-8 **buckle his distempered ... rule:** use the fact he's king to justify his present actions
20 **minutely ... faith-breach:** now there are new rebellions every minute because of his disloyalty (to Duncan and Scotland)
21-2 **move only in command ... love:** obey orders, but don't fight fiercely out of love for him
25 **pestered:** frantic
25 **to recoil and start:** for making him jumpy
26-7 **all that is within ... there?:** he hates himself for what he has become?
29 **the med'cine ... sickly weal:** the medicine that will cure Scotland (Malcolm)
30 **purge:** medicine that cleans the stomach and bowels
32 **dew the sovereign ... weeds:** support the proper ruler (Malcolm) and get rid of these who shouldn't be there (Macbeth and his supporters)

Director's Note, 5.2

✔ An army of Scottish rebels is close to meeting up with Malcolm, Macduff, and the English forces.

✔ They report that Macbeth has few supporters, and he has fortified himself in Dunsinane Castle.

✔ What is significant about Macbeth's choice?

1 **let them fly all:** I don't care if all my nobles desert me
3 **taint:** be stained, corrupted by
5 **All mortal consequences:** everything that will happen on earth
7 **false:** disloyal
8 **epicures:** lovers of luxury, people who live soft lives
9 **The mind I ... bear:** My mind and heart
11 **cream-faced loon:** white faced (with fear) useless, lazy, fool
12 **goose look:** frightened expression

ACT 5 SCENE 3

Servant   There is ten thousand —

Macbeth   Geese, villain?

Servant   Soldiers sir.   15

Macbeth   Go prick thy face and over-red thy fear,
Thou lily-livered boy. What soldiers, patch?
Death of thy soul, those linen cheeks of thine
Are counsellors to fear. What soldiers whey-face?

Servant   The English force, so please you.   20

Macbeth   Take thy face hence.   *[Exit Servant.]*
                Seyton! — I am sick at heart,
When I behold — Seyton, I say! — This push
Will cheer me ever or dis-seat me now.
I have lived long enough. My way of life
Is fallen into the sear, the yellow leaf,   25
And that which should accompany old age,
As honour, love, obedience, troops of friends,
I must not look to have. But in their stead,
Curses, not loud but deep, mouth-honour, breath,
Which the poor heart would fain deny, and dare not. —   30
Seyton!   *Enter Seyton.*

Seyton   What's your gracious pleasure?

Macbeth   What news more?

Seyton   All is confirmed, my lord, which was reported.

Macbeth   I'll fight till from my bones my flesh be hacked.   35
Give me my armour.

Seyton   'Tis not needed yet.

Macbeth   I'll put it on.
Send out more horses, skirr the country round,
Hang those that talk of fear. Give me mine armour. —
How does your patient, doctor?   40

Doctor   Not so sick, my lord,
As she is troubled with thick-coming fancies
That keep her from her rest.

Macbeth   Cure her of that.
Canst thou not minister to a mind diseased,
Pluck from the memory a rooted sorrow;   45
Raze out the written troubles of the brain,
And with some sweet oblivious antidote
Cleanse the stuffed bosom of that perilous stuff
Which weighs upon the heart?

Doctor   Therein the patient must minister to himself.   50

Macbeth   Throw physic to the dogs, I'll none of it. —
Come, put mine armour on. Give me my staff.
Seyton, send out. — Doctor, the Thanes fly from me. —
Come sir, despatch. — If thou couldst, doctor, cast
The water of my land, find her disease,   55

16 **over-red thy fear:** spread the blood on your cheeks to hide your fear
17 **lily-livered:** cowardly
17 **patch:** fool
18 **linen:** white
19 **Are counsellors to fear:** will make everyone else afraid
19 **whey-face:** milk-white

22 **push:** attack
23 **dis-seat me:** push me from my throne

25 **Is fallen ... leaf:** has reached its end, like a dry, yellow leaf
27 **As:** such as
28 **look to have:** expect, hope for
28 **stead:** place
29 **mouth-honour:** insincere flattery
29–30 **breath, Which ... not:** just air, words the speaker wishes he dared not to say

38   **skirr:** scour, search

41–2 **Not so sick ... fancies:** She's not really physically ill, but her mind cannot rest

44 **minister to:** treat, give medicine for
46 **Raze out:** erase
47 **oblivious antidote:** medicine to bring forgetfulness
48–9 **the stuffed bosom ... heart?:** her heart of the dangerous thoughts that fill it?
50 **Therein:** That is something
51 **physic:** medicine
52 **staff:** spear
54 **despatch:** hurry up
54–6 **cast The ... pristine health:** use your skill to diagnose Scotland's problems and cure them

And purge it to a sound and pristine health,
I would applaud thee to the very echo,
That should applaud again. — Pull't off I say. —
What rhubarb, senna, or what purgative drug,
Would scour these English hence? Hear'st thou of them? 60

Doctor   Ay, my good lord. Your royal preparation
Makes us hear something.

Macbeth   Bring it after me.
I will not be afraid of death and bane,
Till Birnam forest come to Dunsinane.

Doctor   [Aside]   Were I from Dunsinane away and clear, 65
Profit again should hardly draw me here.

Exit all.

ACT 5 SCENE 4

*Enter soldiers: a drummer, and others with flags. Then
enter Malcolm, old Siward and his Son, Macduff, Menteith,
Caithness, Angus, Lennox, Ross, and Soldiers marching.*

Malcolm   Cousins, I hope the days are near at hand
That chambers will be safe.

Menteith   We doubt it nothing.

Siward   What wood is this before us?

Meneith   The wood of Birnam. 5

Malcolm   Let every soldier hew him down a bough,
And bear't before him, thereby shall we shadow
The numbers of our host, and make discovery
Err in report of us.

A Soldier   It shall be done.

Siward   We learn no other but the confident tyrant 10
Keeps still in Dunsinane, and will endure
Our setting down before't.

Malcolm   'Tis his main hope.
For where there is advantage to be given,
Both more and less have given him the revolt;
And none serve with him but constrainèd things 15
Whose hearts are absent too.

Macduff   Let our just censures
Attend the true event, and put we on
Industrious soldiership.

Siward   The time approaches, 20
That will with due decision make us know
What we shall say we have and what we owe.
Thoughts speculative their unsure hopes relate,
But certain issue, strokes must arbitrate.
Towards which, advance the war. 25

Exit all, marching.

ACT 5 SCENE 4

59-60 **What rhubarb:** What
medicine?

62 **it:** his armour

65 **Were I:** if only I was

66 **Profit again ... me here:** I
wouldn't come back, no matter
what you paid me

Director's Note, 5.3

Macbeth faces many problems:

✔ the English Army is close

✔ news from the Doctor of Lady Macbeth's
illness.

2 **chambers will be safe:** we'll be
able to sleep safe in our beds

3 **We doubt it nothing:** We don't
doubt it

6 **hew:** cut

7 **shadow:** hide

8 **host:** army

8-9 **discovery Err ... us:** spies give
wrong estimates of our numbers

10 **We learn ... but:** as far as we
can tell

11-2 **Keeps still ... before't:** will
be besieged rather than leave
Dunsinane

13-4 **where there is ... revolt:**
many common people and nobles
have deserted him when they had
the chance

15 **constrainèd things:** those forced
to stay and fight

17-8 **Let our just ... event:** we can
only know the truth of this when
the battle's over

18-9 **put we on ... soldiership:** so
we still need to fight hard and
well

21 **due decision:** once its effects are
assessed

22 **What we shall say ... owe:**
how much of Scotland we truly
possess

23-4 **Thoughts speculative ...
arbitrate:** no point guessing and
hoping, only fighting will give us
the answer

Director's Note, 5.4

✔ The English army and the Scottish rebels have
joined together.

✔ Malcolm's troops to carry branches to hide the
number of men he has, so Birnam Wood seems
to come to Macbeth's castle at Dunsinane.

✔ How does Macbeth react to this evidence of the
Witches' prophesies coming true?

Macbeth and the Messenger, 2013

Which of these lines is a better caption?

a thy story quickly

b The wood began to move / Liar and slave!
Give reasons for your answer.

Joseph Millson, Colin Ryan

Target skill: analysing language

Question: How do lines 15–55 contribute to Shakespeare's presentation of the theme of appearance and reality?

Macbeth's tone of bravado at the start of the scene soon dissipates. On hearing the cry of women he admits that his senses are deadened because he has "supped full with horrors". The proof of this comes in his dulled reaction to news of his wife's death.

Extraordinarily, the play's progress seems almost to pause at this point: Macbeth's wife has just died, he is under attack by an invading English army and deserted by most of his followers, yet he feels that time "creeps in this petty pace from day to day".

Look in pairs at lines 15–27. Remember that in the examination, you are expected to comment on what language does, rather than what it is. You need to comment on the impact particular words and phrases might have on audiences.

- *How would you describe the tone of Macbeth's language in this extract?*
  How might audiences respond to this?
- *Discuss Macbeth's reaction to the news of his wife's death. Does the news affect the rest of his speech?*
- *Talk about the possible impact of the contrasting word length in lines 18 and 19. "There would have been time for such a word" and "Tomorrow and tomorrow and tomorrow".*
- *Discuss the impact that the repetition and the alliteration in this soliloquy might have on an audience.*
- *If you were the director, think what you would say to an actor about the mood that is being conveyed by these lines.*
- Time has been a continual concern for Macbeth. Here he talks of tomorrows. *Discuss what view of time is presented in these lines.*
- *Think and talk about how the image of a "brief candle" links with images elsewhere in the play.*
- *Decide how the image of "a poor player that struts and frets his hour upon the stage" relates to other images of Macbeth's role as king.*
- Shakespeare often uses the theatre as an image of life. *How does he use the image here, and how effective is it?*

FROM THE REHEARSAL ROOM...

LANGUAGE

- In groups of four, read lines 17–28.
- One person reads Macbeth's lines; the other three have listening tasks.
- Person 1 should listen out for repetition.
- Person 2 should listen out for any mentions of time (day, night, hour etc).
- Person 3 listens out for any imagery.
- When the listeners hear what they are listening for (repetition, time or imagery), they repeat the words as soon as the reader has said them.

1 What words are being repeated?

2 What time words are used? Why?

3 What images does Macbeth use?

4 What does repetition, the use of time words, and imagery tell us about Macbeth's state of mind in this scene?

ACT 5 SCENE 5

Enter Macbeth, Seyton and soldiers: a drummer, and others with flags.

Macbeth   Hang out our banners on the outward walls,
The cry is still, "They come:" Our castle's strength
Will laugh a siege to scorn. Here let them lie
Till famine and the ague eat them up.
Were they not forced with those that should be ours,   5
We might have met them dareful, beard to beard,
And beat them backward home.

A cry of women within.

What is that noise?

Seyton   It is the cry of women, my good lord.   *[Exit.]*

Macbeth   I have almost forgot the taste of fears.
The time has been, my senses would have cooled   10
To hear a night-shriek, and my fell of hair
Would at a dismal treatise rouse and stir
As life were in't. I have supped full with horrors,
Direness, familiar to my slaughterous thoughts,
Cannot once start me.   *[Enter Seyton.]*
Wherefore was that cry?   15

Seyton   The queen, my lord, is dead.

Macbeth   She should have died hereafter;
There would have been a time for such a word.
Tomorrow, and tomorrow, and tomorrow,
Creeps in this petty pace from day to day,   20
To the last syllable of recorded time.
And all our yesterdays have lighted fools
The way to dusty death. Out, out, brief candle.
Life's but a walking shadow, a poor player
That struts and frets his hour upon the stage,   25
And then is heard no more. It is a tale
Told by an idiot, full of sound and fury,
Signifying nothing.   *Enter a Messenger.*
Thou com'st to use thy tongue: thy story quickly.

Messenger   Gracious my lord,   30
I should report that which I say I saw,
But know not how to do't.

Macbeth   Well, say sir.

Messenger   As I did stand my watch upon the hill,
I looked toward Birnam, and anon methought   35
The wood began to move.

Macbeth   Liar, and slave!

Messenger   Let me endure your wrath, if't be not so.
Within this three mile may you see it coming.
I say, a moving grove.

Macbeth   If thou speak'st false,

4 **famine and the ague:** starvation and fever
5 **forced with those ... ours:** reinforced with deserters from our side
6 **dareful, beard to beard:** boldly, face to face

10 **The ... been:** once
11–3 **my fell of hair ... were in't:** Then, a scary story would make my hair stand on end
13 **supped full with:** filled myself full of
14 **Direness:** terrible, evil things
15 **once start me:** scare me now
17–8 **She should have ... such a word:** *two possible meanings:* She should have died at a later time, not when I have no time to mourn OR She had to die sometime
20 **this petty pace:** our lives
21 **To the last ... time:** until the end of the world
22–3 **all our yesterdays ... death:** the past shows this to be so
24 **but a walking shadow:** unreal
24 **player:** actor

31–2 **should report ... do't:** don't quite know how to tell you what I saw

34 **did stand my watch:** kept guard
35 **anon:** soon after

39 **grove:** small wood

103

Text focus: Act 5 Scene 5 lines 34–63

Macbeth's lonely defiance of the invading English army has been bolstered by his belief in his own invulnerability. This in turn is based on his trust in the Witches' prophecies, and the news of "a moving grove" begins to undermine that trust.

Macbeth's reign has been disastrous for Scotland and for himself. When he hears of Birnam Wood approaching, he realises that the Witches have duped him, that their words were misleading, and he begins "to pull in resolution" and to "doubt th'equivocation of the fiend that lies like truth."

(AO1) Response to characters and events:

- Despite realising that he has been betrayed by the Witches' words, Macbeth still has his courage when he cries "At least we'll die with harness on our back!" *Do we admire him for his bravery, or did he lose all our sympathy long ago?*

(AO2) Language, structure and form:

- Macbeth's speech is a remarkable combination of three elements:
  i) speaking viciously to the messenger
  ii) soliloquising despairingly as he tries to come to terms with the impossible having happened
  iii) shouting instructions to his soldiers.
  Each element shows us a different aspect of Macbeth. *Which aspect of Macbeth is likely to be most powerful in the mind of the audience?*

(AO3) Context and ideas:

- Regicide has been linked with universal disorder throughout the play. Here Macbeth's world is falling apart, so he explicitly wishes for total chaos in the wider world. *How might an audience react to this wish of Macbeth's?*

Question:

How does Shakespeare present Macbeth's reaction to learning of the Witches' equivocation in lines 35–53?

SHAKESPEARE'S WORLD

FALSE PROPHECIES

People took predicting the future seriously in Shakespeare's time. Both Queen Elizabeth I and King James I used astrologers, and took their advice.

In the world of the play, the Witches seem to predict a future for Macbeth that could never happen. Once the first prophecy comes true, he starts to believe them. His belief is so strong that he bases his decisions on his interpretation of their prophecies.

Many Christians at the time believed that the devil could use false (or misleading) prophecies to tempt people into evil. This is why, when Ross confirms the prophecy that Macbeth will become Thane of Cawdor, Banquo says:

What, can the devil speak true? (Act 1 Scene 3, line 110)

then, later, he says:

And oftentimes, to win us to our harm,

The instruments of darkness tell us truths,

Win us with honest trifles, to betray's

In deepest consequence. (Act 1 Scene 3, lines 127–30)

Banquo was worried that the Witches' prophecies were traps designed to make Macbeth (or him) do terrible things. This question would seem obvious to many people in the original audience. By the end of the play it is clear, his belief in the prophecies has led Macbeth to become a murderer and a tyrant.

Malcolm's army enters through the Yard, spring 2010.

We don't know whether actors entered through the Yard in Shakespeare's time. The only time he specifies where an actor enters from is when the actor is on the upper stage.

Upon the next tree shalt thou hang alive,   40
Till famine cling thee. If thy speech be sooth,
I care not if thou dost for me as much. —
I pull in resolution, and begin
To doubt th' equivocation of the fiend
That lies like truth. "Fear not, till Birnam Wood   45
Do come to Dunsinane", and now a wood
Comes toward Dunsinane. — Arm, arm, and out! —
If this which he avouches does appear,
There is nor flying hence, nor tarrying here.
I 'gin to be a-weary of the sun,   50
And wish th' estate o' the world were now undone. —
Ring the alarum bell! — Blow, wind! come, wrack!
At least we'll die with harness on our back.   *Exit all.*

ACT 5 SCENE 6

Enter soldiers: a drummer, and others with flags, Malcolm,
Siward, Macduff, and their Army, with branches.

Malcolm   Now near enough. Your leafy screens throw down,
And show like those you are. — You, worthy uncle,
Shall with my cousin your right-noble son
Lead our first battle. Worthy Macduff and we
Shall take upon's what else remains to do,   5
According to our order.

Siward   Fare you well.
Do we but find the tyrant's power tonight,
Let us be beaten, if we cannot fight.

Macduff   Make all our trumpets speak, give them all breath,
Those clamorous harbingers of blood and death.   10

The drum plays the call to arms, during which they exit.

ACT 5 SCENE 6

41 **famine cling thee:** you starve to death
41 **sooth:** the truth
42 **pull in resolution:** rein in my certainty
44–5 **th' equivocation … truth:** the promises of the Witches where truth and lies become confused
48 **avouches:** claims to be true
49 **There is nor … tarrying here:** It will be impossible to escape or to stay here
50 **'gin to be … sun:** am getting tired of life
51 **th' estate … now undone:** the world would fall apart
52 **wrack:** revenge
53 **harness:** armour

Director's Note, 5.5

✔ At Dunsinane Macbeth hears Lady Macbeth is dead and a wood seems to approach the castle.
✔ He starts to see the Witches' prophesies do not guarantee success. What does he decide to do?

2 **show like those you are:** let them see what you really are
4 **first battle:** main part of the army
6 **order:** battle plan
7 **Do we but … power:** If we can find Macbeth's army
10 **clamorous harbingers:** loud messengers

SHAKESPEARE'S WORLD

Bear Baiting

Bull and bear baiting were popular entertainments in Shakespeare's London. The main arena was within a couple of hundred yards of the Globe Theatre. The bull or the bear was chained to a stake, and then attacked by fighting dogs. Macbeth invokes this image at the start of Scene 7.

SHAKESPEARE'S WORLD

Sword fighting

A sword was part of an Elizabethan gentleman's elaborate dress. Most gentlemen carried swords in public, and many had a dagger too. The weapons were more a sign of status than for defence. Gentlemen were taught the art of fencing (where the point of the sword, not the edge, was most important).

Actors also trained in sword fighting, and spectacular fights were a feature of many plays. With the exciting swordplay in the last Act, Shakespeare is giving his audience the spectacular action they expected, as well as moving on the main plot. Many modern actors still train in sword fighting, and spectacular fights continue on stage, television and film.

[Photo: Macbeth (James Garnon) fights Young Siward (Shane Zaza), spring 2010 production.]

ACT 5 SCENE 7

Drums offstage play the call to arms, the sounds of a battle. Enter Macbeth.

Macbeth   They have tied me to a stake, I cannot fly,
But, bear-like I must fight the course. What's he
That was not born of woman? Such a one
Am I to fear, or none.

Enter Young Siward.

Young Siward   What is thy name?   5

Macbeth   Thou'lt be afraid to hear it.

Young Siward   No, though thou call'st thyself a hotter name
Than any is in hell.

Macbeth   My name's Macbeth.

Young Siward   The devil himself could not pronounce a title
More hateful to mine ear.   10

1–2 **They have tied ... course:** I'm trapped, like a bear being baited (see box opposite).

2–3 **What's he That ... woman?:** What sort of man could possibly not be born from a woman?

Macbeth	No, nor more fearful.	
Young Siward	Thou liest, abhorred tyrant, with my sword I'll prove the lie thou speak'st.	12 **abhorred:** hated, loathed

They fight, Young Siward is killed.

Macbeth	Thou wast born of woman. But swords I smile at, weapons laugh to scorn, 15 Brandished by man that's of a woman born. *Exit.*	

Drums offstage play the call to arms, the sounds of a battle.
Enter Macduff.

Macduff	That way the noise is. Tyrant show thy face! If thou be'st slain and with no stroke of mine, My wife and children's ghosts will haunt me still. I cannot strike at wretched kerns, whose arms 20 Are hired to bear their staves; either thou, Macbeth, Or else my sword with an unbattered edge I sheathe again undeeded. There thou shouldst be, By this great clatter, one of greatest note Seems bruited. Let me find him Fortune, 25 And more I beg not. *Exit.*	18 **with no stroke of mine:** not by me 20-1 **kerns, whose arms ... staves:** hired foot soldiers 22 **unbattered:** unused 23 **undeeded:** without having used it 24-5 **By this great ... bruited:** someone important must be fighting where all that noise is

Drums offstage play the call to arms, the sounds of a battle.
Enter Malcolm and Siward.

Siward	This way, my lord, the castle's gently rendered. The tyrant's people on both sides do fight, The noble thanes do bravely in the war, The day almost itself professes yours, 30 And little is to do.	27 **gently rendered:** given up, without much resistance 30 **The day almost ... yours:** we have as good as won
Malcolm	We have met with foes That strike beside us.	32-3 **We have met ... beside us:** Our enemies have changed sides to fight with us
Siward	Enter, sir, the castle.	

They exit. Drums offstage play the call to arms, the sounds
of a battle. Enter Macbeth.

Macbeth	Why should I play the Roman fool, and die 35 On mine own sword? Whiles I see lives, the gashes Do better upon them.	35 **the Roman fool:** some Roman generals committed suicide when defeated 36 **lives:** living enemies

Enter Macduff.

Macduff	Turn hell-hound, turn!	
Macbeth	Of all men else I have avoided thee. But get thee back, my soul is too much charg'd With blood of thine already. 40	38 **Of all men else:** More than any other man 39 **charg'd:** weighed down with 40 **blood of thine:** your family's blood
Macduff	I have no words, My voice is in my sword, thou bloodier villain Than terms can give thee out. *They fight. Alarum.*	43 **terms can give thee out:** words can say
Macbeth	Thou losest labour. As easy may'st thou the intrenchant air 45 With thy keen sword impress, as make me bleed.	44 **losest labour:** are wasting your time 45 **intrenchant:** uncuttable 46 **keen:** sharp 46 **impress:** make a mark on

Let fall thy blade on vulnerable crests,
I bear a charmèd life, which must not yield
To one of woman born.

Macduff   Despair thy charm,
And let the angel whom thou still hast served
Tell thee, Macduff was from his mother's womb   50
Untimely ripped.

Macbeth   Accursèd be that tongue that tells me so,
For it hath cowed my better part of man.
And be these juggling fiends no more believed   55
That palter with us in a double sense,
That keep the word of promise to our ear
And break it to our hope. I'll not fight with thee.

Macduff   Then yield thee, coward,
And live to be the show and gaze o' th' time.   60
We'll have thee, as our rarer monsters are,
Painted upon a pole, and underwrit,
"Here may you see the tyrant."

Macbeth   I will not yield
To kiss the ground before young Malcolm's feet,   65
And to be baited with the rabble's curse.
Though Birnam wood be come to Dunsinane,
And thou opposed, being of no woman born,
Yet I will try the last. Before my body,
I throw my warlike shield. Lay on, Macduff,   70
And damned be him that first cries "Hold, enough!"

*They exit, fighting. Drums offstage play the call to arms, the
sounds of a battle.
Re-enter Macbeth and Macduff, fighting. Macbeth is killed.
Macduff exits, with Macbeth's body.*

47 **vulnerable crests:** the heads of men who can be wounded
49 **Despair thy charm:** your magic protection is worthless
50 **angel:** evil guiding spirit
52 **Untimely ripped:** born by Caesarian operation, not born naturally
54 **cowed my ... man:** taken away my courage
55–6 **juggling fiends ... double sense:** Witches who deceive us by using double meaning
57–8 **keep the word ... hope:** make promises that seem true but let us down
60 **show and gaze ... time:** a public amusement for many years
62 **Painted upon ... underwrit:** with your picture on a sign outside the sideshow tent that says
66 **baited with the rabble's curse:** shown off for the public to curse
68 **thou opposed:** you, my opponent
69 **try the last:** fight to the end
69 **before:** in front of
70 **Lay on:** Let's go
71 **Hold, enough:** Stop, I give in

Director's Note, 5.7

✔ In the battle, Macduff searches for Macbeth.

✔ Macduff tells Macbeth he was not "of woman born". They fight, and Macduff kills him.

exam SKILLS

Target skill: analysing the denouement

Question: How do lines 35–71 contribute to Shakespeare's final presentation of Macbeth?

Remember that a play is not just a story. This is the denouement (the dramatic conclusion) that Shakespeare has prepared the audience for from the beginning. The words given to Banquo in Act I, that "the instruments of darkness tell us truths, win us with honest trifles to betray's in deepest consequence" were an early signal that things would not end well for Macbeth. His life's trajectory, once he had killed for the crown, was inevitably downwards.

After the short scenes of hectic warfare, this is when Macbeth, recognising that he has lost the battle, contemplates but rejects suicide and expresses regret (for the first time) over murdering Macduff's family. He finally realises

that the Witches are "juggling fiends" who "keep the word of promise to our ear and break it to our hope", but fights on regardless.

- In pairs, look for and list the terms Macduff uses to describe Macbeth. *Do they confirm or challenge your view of Macbeth?*
- Macduff claims that "my voice is in my sword". *How do his speeches differ from Macbeth's?*
- Compare the tone of Macbeth's speech beginning "Thou losest labour" with his next speech which begins "Accursed..." *What differences do you notice?*
- In his last speech Macbeth, having listed the ways the Witches have betrayed him, still cries, "Yet I will try the last". *What are your hopes for him as he leaves the stage still battling with Macduff?*

ACT 5 SCENE 8

Drums play the Retreat, then Trumpets a fanfare. Enter Soldiers with drum and flags, then Malcolm, Siward, Ross, Thanes, and Soldiers.

Malcolm   I would the friends we miss were safe arrived.

Siward   Some must go off: and yet by these I see,
So great a day as this is cheaply bought.

Malcolm   Macduff is missing, and your noble son.

Ross   Your son, my lord, has paid a soldier's debt,   5
He only lived but till he was a man,
The which no sooner had his prowess confirmed
In the unshrinking station where he fought,
But like a man he died.

Siward   Then is he dead?

Ross   Ay, and brought off the field. Your cause of sorrow   10
Must not be measured by his worth, for then
It hath no end.

Siward   Had he his hurts before?

Ross   Ay, on the front.

Siward   Why then, God's soldier be he.
Had I as many sons as I have hairs,   15
I would not wish them to a fairer death:
And so his knell is knolled.

Malcolm   He's worth more sorrow,
And that I'll spend for him.

Siward   He's worth no more.
They say he parted well, and paid his score,
And so God be with him. — Here comes newer comfort.   20

Enter Macduff, with Macbeth's head.

Macduff   Hail, king, for so thou art. Behold, where stands
The usurper's cursed head. The time is free.
I see thee compassed with thy kingdom's pearl,
That speak my salutation in their minds;
Whose voices I desire aloud with mine.   25
Hail, King of Scotland!

All   Hail, King of Scotland!

Fanfare of trumpets.

Malcolm   We shall not spend a large expense of time
Before we reckon with your several loves,
And make us even with you. My thanes and kinsmen,
Henceforth be earls, the first that ever Scotland   30
In such an honour named. What's more to do,
Which would be planted newly with the time,
As calling home our exiled friends abroad
That fled the snares of watchful tyranny,

1 **I would:** If only
1 **we miss:** who aren't here
2 **must go off:** must be dead
2–3 **by these I see ... bought:** seeing who is here, you've lost very few to win a great victory
5 **paid a soldier's debt:** died in battle
7–8 **The which ... fought:** and as soon as he had proved he was a man by fighting well and bravely
10–1 **cause of sorrow ... worth:** grief must not be as great as his nobility
16 **I would ... death:** I couldn't hope for a better death for them
17 **And so his knell is knolled:** And that's his epitaph
19 **parted:** died
19 **paid his score:** did his duty (literally, paid his bills)
20 **newer comfort:** more up-to-date and cheering news
22 **The usurper:** the person who stole your throne (Macbeth)
22 **The time:** now we are
23 **compassed:** surrounded by
23 **pearl:** best nobles
24–5 **That speak ... with mine:** who I know agree with me and I ask them to join me in saying
28–9 **reckon with your ... with you:** reward you for your support
30 **Henceforth:** From now on
32 **Which would be ... time:** to make a fresh start
33 **As:** includes
34 **snares:** traps
34 **watchful tyranny:** Macbeth's spies

Director's Note, 5.8

✔ Malcolm won the battle. Macduff brings him Macbeth's head.
✔ Malcolm rewards his followers by making some of them Earls.

Producing forth the cruel ministers 35
Of this dead butcher and his fiend-like queen
(Who, as 'tis thought, by self and violent hands,
Took off her life). This, and what needful else
That calls upon us, by the grace of Grace,
We will perform in measure, time and place. 40
So thanks to all at once and to each one,
Whom we invite to see us crowned at Scone.

A trumpet fanfare. *Exit all.*

35 **Producing forth:** finding
35 **ministers:** servants, officials
37-8 **by self and violent ... life:** committed suicide
38-9 **what needful ... upon us:** any other duties I must carry out
39 **by the grace of Grace:** with God's help
40 **measure, time and place:** carefully, at the right time and in the right place

Macduff displays Macbeth's head. Malcolm, with his back to us.

What did Shakespeare do at the end of the fight (page 106), to set up this moment?

Nicholas Khan, Philip Cumbus

1.1	A storm. Three Witches plan to meet Macbeth.
1.2	King Duncan hears that his army has defeated the rebels. He has the Thane of Cawdor, who betrayed him, executed and will give his title to Macbeth.
1.3	The Witches tell Macbeth he will become Thane of Cawdor and then king. They tell Banquo his sons will be kings. Ross arrives and informs Macbeth he is Thane of Cawdor. Macbeth starts to think about becoming king.
1.4	Duncan praises Macbeth and Banquo, names Malcolm as the next king, and plans to visit Macbeth in his castle.
1.5	Lady Macbeth reads a letter from Macbeth telling her about the Witches. When he arrives, she persuades him to murder Duncan.
1.6	Lady Macbeth welcomes Duncan and his court.
1.7	Macbeth decides not to murder Duncan; Lady Macbeth changes his mind.
2.1	Macbeth meets Banquo and his son, Fleance. After they go, he is troubled, and thinks he sees a dagger leading him to Duncan's room.
2.2	Macbeth has killed Duncan but does not leave the daggers. Lady Macbeth takes them back to implicate the grooms. Somebody knocks at the gate.
2.3	The Porter lets in Macduff and Lennox. Macduff discovers Duncan is dead. Macbeth kills the grooms. Duncan's sons flee.
2.4	Macduff reports the belief that the grooms killed Duncan, that Duncan's sons have fled, and that Macbeth has been chosen king.
3.1	Banquo suspects Macbeth. Macbeth plans to murder Banquo and Fleance.
3.2	Macbeth does not tell Lady Macbeth his plan to have Banquo murdered.
3.3	The murderers kill Banquo, but Fleance escapes.
3.4	At a banquet, Macbeth (and only Macbeth) sees Banquo's ghost. His reaction unsettles his guests. He decides to re-visit the Witches.
3.5	Hecate tells the Witches their prophecies will destroy Macbeth.
3.6	Lennox and a Lord discuss their suspicions of Macbeth, and report that Macduff has gone to England to join Malcolm, who is raising an army.
4.1	The Witches show Macbeth apparitions, whose promises convince him he is safe unless Birnam Wood comes to Dunsinane and he can't be harmed by one 'of woman born'. He orders the killing of Macduff's family.
4.2	Macbeth's men murder Lady Macduff and her children.
4.3	Macduff joins Malcolm in England. Ross arrives with news of the murder of Macduff's family. They agree to invade Scotland with the help of England.
5.1	Lady Macbeth is observed by a Doctor and a Gentlewoman walking in her sleep.
5.2	Malcolm's army invades, and Scottish rebels join him.
5.3	Macbeth's supporters are deserting. The doctor cannot cure Lady Macbeth.
5.4	Malcolm orders his soldiers to cut branches from Birnam Wood to use as camouflage as they move to attack Macbeth in Dunsinane Castle.
5.5	Macbeth is told of his wife's death, and that a wood seems to be advancing on the castle. He starts to doubt the Witches' prophecies.
5.6	Malcolm's army attacks.
5.7	Macbeth kills Young Siward, but is killed by Macduff.
5.8	Malcolm is proclaimed king.

Key terms

These key terms provide a starting place for exploring key aspects of *Macbeth*.

THEMES AND IDEAS

Ambition/power

The Witches rouse Macbeth's ambition to be king 1.3.51; 1.3.148–9; 1.4. 48–52; but it's balanced by his view of honour 1.7. 12–28 Lady Macbeth's ambition influences Macbeth to murder Duncan 1.7, 2.2; Macbeth's ambition then leads to more murder and his death 3.1. 124–155; 4.1. 154–9; 4.2; 5.7. 70

Appearance and reality

Hypocrisy and deception of the Macbeths: The Macbeths make loyal speeches while plotting against Duncan 1.4. 22–27 (1.6. 15–21); 1.7. 82–3; Lady Macbeth tells Macbeth to 'Look like th'innocent flower/ But be the serpent under't' 1.5. 64–5; before killing Duncan, Macbeth says they must sustain their false show of honouring him 1.7. 82–3; Lady Macbeth daubs Duncan's blood on servants to incriminate them 2.2.62–67; both pretend shock when the body is found 2.3; Macbeth appears friendly to Banquo while plotting his murder 3.1. 11–47; when Macbeth sees Banquo's ghost, and talks to it, Lady Macbeth says he has a recurring illness 3.4

Supernatural appearances: Macbeth's vision of the dagger 2.1. 41–49; Banquo's ghost 3.4; Banquo's eight royal descendants 4.1.115–128

Witches' appearances and deception: the seeming promise of good fortune in new titles for Macbeth 1.3. 49–51; the prophecies that 'show' Macbeth can never be vanquish'd 4.1. 83–98; deception revealed 5.5. 33; 5.7.48–52

Choices

Macbeth chooses to let the Witches influence him 1.3.131–150, 1.4. 48–51, 3.4.141–3, 4.1. 47; Banquo is wary of the Witches and warns against them 1.3. 126–130;

Lady Macbeth influences Macbeth to murder Duncan 1.7; Macbeth chooses to murder Duncan 1.7. 80–83, Banquo 3.1. 124–155 and Macduffs 4.1. 155–9; Lady Macbeth's choices: guilt/sleepwalking 5.1; her death/supposed suicide 5.5. 16/5.8.36–38

Conflict/Good and evil

Conflicting views of the Witches: Banquo 1.3. 126–30; Macbeth 1.3. 134–146

Conflict within a character: Macbeth and his conscience before murdering Duncan 1.7. 1–28 and after 2.2 27–87

Conflict within the Macbeths' marriage: e.g. before the murder of Duncan 1.7. 35–83

Conflict as Macbeth's evil grows: Banquo's murder 3.1; Macduff and others turn against him 4.1. 146; murders Macduff family 4.1. 149–161; 4.2

Equivocation/Ambiguity

The Witches equivocate with 'Fair is foul, and foul is fair' 1.1. 11; Macbeth's first words echo this equivocation which creates a link with the Witches 1.3. 39

Equivocation used to mislead: e.g. the Witches promise Macbeth he cannot be harmed by anyone of woman born not saying Macduff was born by caesarean section 4.1. 83

Equivocation used to create dramatic irony: e.g. Macbeth says when he hears of Duncan's death: 'Had I but died an hour before this chance, I had lived a blessed time.' 2.3. 95–6 Ross tells Macduff: 'they were well at peace, when I did leave 'em', suggesting all's well – then explains they are dead 4.3. 198

Guilt

Macbeth feels guilt: e.g. after murdering Duncan 2.2. 27–87, with Banquo's ghost 3.4. 55–149 and fighting Macduff 5.7. 38–41; *Lady Macbeth's guilt:* leads to sleepwalking and trying to wash Duncan's blood from her hands 5.1. 32–48, 64–71; 5.5, 5.8. 36–8

Hero/tragic hero

Macbeth is first presented a hero: 1.2; he becomes a tragic hero (because of his actions or what is done to him); e.g. ambition 1.3; 2.2; 3.3; the Witches' influence 4.1; 4.2; Macbeth realises he has been deceived 5.7. 71–end

Justice/judgement

Macbeth fears human justice and God's justice 1.7. 1–25; his evil deeds are challenged by Banquo's ghost 3.4. 38–149; Lady Macbeth is overwhelmed by guilt 5.1; 5.5. 16; 5.8. 36–8; Macduff kills Macbeth 5.7; The restoration of King Malcolm 5.8. 21–42

Kingship

Macbeth says Duncan's a good King so it is wrong to be disloyal 1.7. 16–20; Macbeth seizes power from Duncan's named heir, Malcolm 2.3.143–149; 2.4.27–35; Macbeth's kingship contrasts with Malcolm's kingly behaviour 4.1; 5.8. 27–42

Male/female

The Witches' gender is disordered 1.3. 46–48; Lady Macbeth rejects her femininity 1.5. 36–52; 1.7. 54–9; says Macbeth is 'too full o' th' milk of human kindness' to kill and unmanly 1.5. 14–28; Macbeth sees killing in battle as manly, but murder as unmanly 1.7. 46–7; sees his visions of Banquo as a 'feminine' weakness 3.4. 64–73; Macduff says grief and revenge are manly 4.3. 245–62

Supernatural

The influence of the supernatural: the Witches' appearances, spells and prophecies: 1.1, 1.3, 3.5, 4.1 and their fulfilment 1.3, 5.5, 5.7; after Duncan's murder the natural world behaves unnaturally 2.3.52–63; 2.4.1–23

Macbeth sees supernatural apparitions: e.g. a dagger 2.1. 41–72, Banquo's ghost 3.4 and the future kings 4.1

LANGUAGE

Alliteration

Repetition of the same consonant sounds, especially at the beginning of words; e.g. 'Go get some water, And wash this filthy witness from your hand' 2.2. 55–56

Assonance

Repetition of vowel sounds to make a line sound longer or more emotional: 'What thou wouldst highly,/That wouldst thou holily; wouldst not play false,/And yet wouldst wrongly win.' 1.5. 18–20

Blank verse

Verse which does not have lines ending with rhyming words or a set pattern of lines to a verse. It has a regular pattern of stresses sometimes leaving out the syllables of ordinary speech; e.g. 'I will advise you where to plant yourselves,/ Acquaint you with the perfect spy o'th' time,/The moment on't, for't must be done tonight' 3.1. 141–3

Imagery

Language which creates vivid, usually visual, images – particularly if Shakespeare is describing something that can't be shown on stage, e.g. the metaphor: 'full of scorpions is my mind' 3.2.39

Animal imagery: Shakespeare refers to savage animals (e.g. wolves 2.1. 61) to suggest violence; and gentle animals (e.g. 'the poor cat in the adage' 1.7. 45) to suggest harmlessness.

Blood imagery: Used to convey violence and destruction e.g. first description of Macbeth 1.2. 15–23 a symbol for Macbeth's guilt 3.4. 145–7; and reluctance to fight Macduff 5.7. 38–40

Night/darkness imagery: suggest danger and hidden intentions, as in Lady Macbeth's 'Come thick night,/And pall thee in the dunnest smoke of hell' 1.5. 48–9; after Duncan dies, day is dark as night 2.5. 11, 2.4. 8

Pentameters/broken pentameters

These are the two-syllable units of a ten-syllable line e.g. 2.2. 11 'Alack – I am – afraid – they have – awaked.'

Prose

Everyday speech is often given to low-class characters, such as the Porter 2.3

Rhyme rhythm

Shakespeare uses a regular beat or stress of syllables in a line to create a ritual effect, as with the Witches. He also uses rhyme to help an actor remember lines and breathe while speaking them e.g. 'O, **full** of **scorp**ions is my **mind**, dear **wife**' 3.4. 39. He also uses couplets to show a scene is coming to an end e.g. 3.2. 55–8